How to Complain [More]
EFFECTIVELY

How to Complain [More]
EFFECTIVELY

Charles M. Dobbs

authorHOUSE®

AuthorHouse™
1663 Liberty Drive
Bloomington, IN 47403
www.authorhouse.com
Phone: 1-800-839-8640

Published by AuthorHouse 11/11/2014

ISBN: 978-1-4969-5269-1 (sc)
ISBN: 978-1-4969-5268-4 (e)

Library of Congress Control Number: 2014920207

TABLE OF CONTENTS

CHAPTER ONE

Introduction

You purchase a food item at the grocery and when you prepare it at home, it did not come out or taste like the advertisement promised.

You visit a store intending to purchase an item you saw on a national advertisement – on television or in a newspaper insert – and the store clerk informs you that price is not valid.

You fill out the form for a rebate on a purchase and weeks later you learn the company claims you did not qualify and denies your rebate.

You see several people in line ahead of you receiving good treatment from a store employee yet you receive different treatment and wonder why?

You call the toll free customer service line and either the constant automatic diverting [it's not really an answering] system wears you down or the representative, when you finally reach a representative, cannot give you satisfaction.

I'm sure it has happened to you. You were dissatisfied with some interaction – perhaps something you purchased, perhaps a service you received, perhaps a promise not fulfilled or not fulfilled as you had expected. Depending on your personality, you may have felt stressed; you may have wanted to throttle someone; you may have done something you later regretted, yelling at someone and all too often at the wrong someone.

And what did you do afterwards to relieve this stress and gain resolution or satisfaction?

Most folks complain – to their friends, to their family, to their co-workers. Some will yell and I do mean yell – lose their composure – at store personnel or at a customer service representative over the telephone. Few take time to complain to the organization that dissatisfied them. Some keep it to themselves and let the occurrence eat away at them, increasing their stress; and fewer of them complain effectively. And, when you failed to gain the satisfaction you wanted, you were even more dissatisfied.

You did not complain effectively and, more importantly, you did not complain effectively to the right people. Most employees in most organizations have to follow the rules and must say "no" to your request for "yes." Individual employees cannot make individual rules to resolve individual complaints; organizations need broad, consistent operating rules that cover the majority of situations. But every organization has a few people who have the authority, the experience, and hopefully the judgment to make exceptions. You need to understand therefore what to do and how to do it and to whom to send it to obtain the satisfaction you want.

I want to help you learn how to complain effectively. Actually, I want to help you complain *more* effectively. Please note: you are not doing this to vent; you are not doing this to force a company to compensate you out of fear of embarrassment, negative publicity, or simply the time it takes to deal with a complainant. You are doing it because you strongly believe something went wrong and you want the company leadership to know about it and to remedy it. In a larger sense, if done correctly, complaining helps an organization improve itself. Good organizations are committed to the process of continual improvement, and need your feedback and that of others to continue to improve. Good CEOs lead such good organizations and value your feedback if given appropriately, informatively, and politely. What better way to improve than to obtain feedback from end users like you?

CHAPTER TWO

My previous history with complain letters

Where it all began for me

I was either fourteen or fifteen years old [I don't remember any more] and we were living in Stamford, Connecticut in the mid-1960s. My mother bought a raisin pound cake from a well-known and highly-regarded American baked goods company, and she served us each a slice for dessert. This was a real treat – for we only had dessert once a week and it was good. As luck would have it, I found what I thought was a wooden match stick [without the match head] in my slice. I showed it to my father, who said, well, "write the company a letter."

I assume he figured I would say yes but I'd forget about it. Nope. I had taken a typing class that previous summer and I wanted to show off my new skills; I wrote to the address on the container. I explained that we had dessert once a week, and we all looked forward to it. This one particular time there was this wooden match stick in the batter which I enclosed. I suggested – as a teenager no less – that perhaps the company president should check quality control at the bakery and make sure that the company's bakers weren't smoking on the job [and tossing the match sticks into the batter].

About a week later I received a wonderful written response from the corporate offices explaining that my "find" was a raisin stem that somehow survived the process of separating raisins from the stems; perhaps that was true and perhaps it was a match stick! Nonetheless, the letter noted the CEO felt badly, and that evening a nice young man in his 20s showed up at our house with several different dessert products the company produced by way of apology.

I wrote a brief, polite, to the point letter, and the company – a great American success story – to its great credit responded appropriately. By the way, what a great job!

He said he had a partner, and they had southern Fairfield County, Connecticut as their area of responsibility to call on such letter writers at their homes to give away Sara Lee product [and products of other companies that they also represented] when something had gone awry. Apparently, they tested the products more than occasionally before taking them to dissatisfied customers; he seemed a rather happy fellow ☺. I don't remember the guidance counselors at Rippowam High School telling us about that option on career day!

On the other hand, in April 2012 my wife and I returned to the Des Moines International Airport from a brief trip to Connecticut. As we were waiting for our suitcase at baggage claim, I heard – everyone in the cavernous baggage claim area heard – a passenger from our flight yelling at a baggage claim staffer of a large American air carrier, the sole airline baggage employee in a small, regional airport. Apparently he was mad at the airline for not sending him from Chicago [where our flight originated] to his desired destination – Hartford, Connecticut. Instead, something went wrong, and he boarded – the airline put him on – a flight for his home airport, Des Moines.

Who knows who was at fault, but what good did it do him to yell at a young woman who was covering the baggage claim area in Des Moines? If he really wanted to get to Hartford, the solution to his problem was in Chicago where he was and from where that airline flew regularly and frequently to Hartford, not in Des Moines, an airport so small that it was served by the company's affiliate flying so-called commuter jets and not the main company with its full-sized passenger jets. And why yell at a young woman who neither was responsible for the problem nor could not provide a solution? [To her credit, she called for the airline's station master at the airport in Des Moines to speak with the irate passenger, but, he was wrong, wrong, wrong.]

And, while on the subject, **one needs to learn to fight in one's weight class**. Don't yell at an entry level staffer because, frankly, she or he is available and has to be polite despite your misdirected rage. Don't yell at a secretary or a desk clerk or any similar person. It won't move you to resolution of the issue. It only proves you are a boor and a bully. And, in many organizations, you would have lost your chance for a resolution to your issue by such boorish behavior.

Your grandmother was right . . . you'll catch more flies with honey than vinegar. Be nice.

WORKING ON THE OTHER SIDE

I worked as the assistant to the president at two universities for a total of fifteen years [time away from honest work as a history faculty member which I did for twenty-two more years! ☺]. During that time, I never liked when someone would call or come to our offices and yell at secretaries. They were all good people; they all meant well. None of them was paid enough to take such crap and none of them had the authority to resolve the situation if, indeed, it merited resolution from either university. As fast as I could, I would come out of my office, grab that secretary's telephone or come out into the main office, and begin by telling the caller who I was and then indicating it was inappropriate to yell at a staff member. There was no reason, no justification for abusing a staff person. **Again, fight in your own weight class.** Or, in this case, yell at me for I was paid more appropriately to take such crap. [No one is paid enough for such crap, but I was better paid than they were.]

I write this book because of these twin experiences. I have always been willing to write a complaint letter when I have been disappointed. I like the discipline of writing. It probably reflects my vocation, for I am a history professor and I like the task of gathering my facts, organizing my argument, suggesting a resolution, and sending the letter.

I have had great success when I was right and I had my facts in proper order, correcting situations that bothered me. Also, I write fan letters when something extremely nice happens – it's seems like a kind of karma; I bank the afterglow of a positive letter I write to use when I am disappointed and write a negative letter. Also, I believe one has to praise good service to earn the right to criticize poor service or a poor product. It's only right.

As mentioned above, I strayed from my honest work as a faculty member to serve for fifteen years as the Executive Assistant to the President at Metropolitan State University of Denver and Iowa State University. Among many, other duties, I was the final, informal complaint resolution officer for each institution. If someone was right; if the institution had acted incorrectly, I wanted to correct the situation. Frankly my resolving it occurred at a lot lower and less expensive level than calling in the attorneys for either side.

To be sure, most times most organizations and companies act appropriately and I was very willing to explain what had occurred, correct the error of fact or misinterpretation the complainant had and defend why I had concluded that the institution and its representatives had acted correctly. And I never liked people, regardless of how badly they felt the institution had treated them, who beat on folks who could not respond in kind – secretaries, part-time student employees [think the front desk person in a Student Financial Aid office or a campus housing office], etc. **Again, fight in your own weight class.**

I certainly wanted to help correct institutional errors where there were such errors, and I believe so do organizational and corporate CEOs. They also need to know if there is a problem with some part of their operation. Everyone makes a mistake once in a while; but, if a unit keeps making the same mistake or failing to provide the service for which that unit exists, then it is time for corrective action. An appropriate complaint helps make organizations more efficient.

Two examples:

A student, his parents, and his grandparents came to see the president at Metro State which meant, of course, they had to speak with me. His family had traveled some distance to see him graduate that May and, literally at the last moment, he learned he had failed to meet a university requirement. It was stupid. He had taken an English Composition course at an AAU institution [that is, one of the top 60 research universities in the United States] and the English Department at my institution [which was not an AAU university] did not think that course measured up to its standards or so he explained to me.

I called the department chair and asked about the situation, and then asked how quickly did she let this student [and, for that matter, other students] know about the department's decision not to permit the transfer course to meet the composition requirement for graduation. She responded that she signed a letter for the student to pick up in the department office.

Did students know they had to come get the letter, I asked? She did not know; there was a wicker basket full of such letters in the English Department main office. Bingo! I wrote what in Colorado was called an "error message" for the file, waived the requirement in this specific case only, and let the young man graduate. He had taken an equivalent course and if it wasn't equivalent the department had two years to contact him and let him know he had to take its own version of English composition to meet the requirement. Thereafter, I wrote the arts and sciences dean, described what had occurred, and suggested he discuss good administrative procedures with his department chairs or, barring that, this specific chair.

More recently, parents called the president's office at ISU to complain on behalf of their child. It would have been better for the child to complain on his own. However, I listened and they indicated his academic advisor had recommended he take the most difficult of three general chemistry sequences. They thought he was not prepared for that challenge, and, as it turned out, he did not do all that well and dropped the course. I checked with a few academic advisors I knew and they agreed given the situation I described they would not have signed the student into that demanding sequence.

I made my decision. I spoke with the Financial Aid Director, a good person, and asked if we could set up a non-refundable tuition scholarship for the amount of the dropped course for the student to use in his next semester. The advisor was a highly regarded, long serving member of the university and he felt terrible about what happened; I saw no reason to embarrass him, but I wanted to make the student whole again. The FinAid director agreed; we contacted the student; he was pleased and the parents wrote a thank you note to the president.

Our children have watched me complain over the years and they act in such situations much as I do. [Sometimes it is rather scary to see how much one's children are like oneself and vice versa!] Our son called one day to tell us of an experience he had at a popular, mid-priced mall clothing store. He was standing in line, and several young women ahead of him completed their respective purchases. In each case, they produced a debit or credit card, swiped it, received their receipt, and left with their purchases. When it was his turn, the clerk asked him for additional identification. He asked why she was treating him differently and then asked to speak with the store manager. He wanted to know from the manager why that store employee had treated him very differently. A few minutes later he left the store with his purchase gifted him by the store manager.

Jonathan only asked why the clerk had differentiated and what was the store policy on such individual decision making; he did not threaten; he did not yell; he was clear, brief, insistent, and polite. The store manager corrected the situation and Jonathan was satisfied. Kudos to the store manager of this clothing store at a large regional mall in eastern, Iowa for making the proverbial lemonade from lemons. Hopefully, he followed up with a training session for cashiers and the front area lead employee.

Similarly, our daughter was buying a sandwich at a popular sandwich chain outlet in downtown Dallas, Texas. Hannah clearly indicated to the servers making the sandwich that she liked to watch her weight and not eat unnecessary excess fat – such as mayonnaise, salad oil or cheese. She noted what she did not want on the sandwich. This chain has a high counter so she could not see what the sandwich makers were doing. After returning to her office, she found the sandwich had the very fat and calories she did not want and had explicitly asked the counter staff to leave out. By the way, as an attorney, she certainly expresses herself clearly.

She sent an e-mail to the chain, explained the situation, and expressed her disappointment. The next day the local store manager called, apologized, and provided her with several coupons for free sandwiches. Hannah was satisfied. Hopefully, that store manager used this experience as a means to discuss with the store staff of the need to listen to customers. And, kudos to the sandwich chain for promptly responding to a valid customer complaint. Good job!

On the other hand, I did a turn as History Department chair. [There was a lot of arm twisting, undeserved praise of my administrative abilities, and politely worded threats from the dean and I caved in.] One day I received an e-mail from someone who identified himself as the father of a current history major. He wrote to complain – rather threateningly and certainly rudely by the way – that we – it was not clear if the "we" was the History Department specifically or the university more generally – would not let his son graduate even though the son had been a student at the University for six years.

On the surface, this made no sense, and I looked into the matter [which really means I asked our department's outstanding academic advisor about the student and his circumstances]. Most American universities and colleges require students to petition, to file for graduation. Even if a student meets a set of requirements, he or she needs to "ask" to graduate. Perhaps the student wishes a second major, an additional minor field, an internship, a study abroad, or an area of certification.

The young man in question had more than 180 valid college credit hours, reflecting six years in college; he fulfilled all the requirements for graduation; his grade point average more than exceeded the university's minimum for graduation. However, he apparently had no interest in graduating, had never applied to the Registrar to graduate, **and he had the right to stay in school as long as he wanted**.

Father needed to have an honest conversation with his son, including a clear discussion of the parents' obligation to help finance the education; the father could not resolve the situation – having his son graduate – by writing an e-mail to yell at me. By the way, given so-called student privacy legislation, I did not have the right to explain the situation to the father although in responding to his e-mail by e-mail I did create a theoretical situation that was darned close to his son's situation and tried to alert the father about the truth of his son's situation. But from his e-mail reply he clearly did not want to listen to me and continued to blame us – the History Department faculty – for his son's lengthy time in school. What a waste of his time and mine!

In another example, a graduate of my department sent a complaint letter to the University president and the alumni association president that she had graduated with a bachelor's degree in history and did not have a job several months later. Of course, the two presidents bumped the issue to me [she did not write nor copy me as department chair on the complaint]. In looking into the situation, baccalaureate degrees in the humanities are not "finishing" degrees; they are not the equivalent of a degree in engineering or agronomy; most students go on and secure teaching licensure or enter law school, library school, or graduate school in history. And, in her case, she had interacted with the college's fine career services web site for a grand total of **seven seconds**! Since the site required students to log in, the site also recorded time on the site. And, of course, she tried not to meet with the department advisor who would have happily given her accurate and useful career advice.

I wrote all this in my response, and copied the two presidents. She responded that I was right, and she realized she did not take advantage of the resources Iowa State offered. She admitted she wrote only because she was frustrated as her school loans came due. Why take it out on the terrific department academic advisor? Why not call the career services office and although somewhat belatedly see what assistance it could provide in her job search?

So, you have your choice. Learn the right way to complain and most times you will receive satisfaction because most organizations want to do right. More than forty years ago, Robert Townsend, who served for several years as CEO of Avis-Rent-A-Car when it premiered its wonderful "We're only #2, so we try harder" campaign, wrote *Up the Organization*. The book was and is full of wisdom for corporate CEOs, but his comment about firing the corporate PR operation has always stuck in my mind. He said that the way receptionists and others – first greeters he called them – greeted the public made corporate public relations. It was a smart point, and hopefully most American companies continue to agree with Mr. Townsend. While such "front desk" employees represent the company, they usually cannot right wrongs even if they agree something is wrong.

Or continue to complain inappropriately and ineffectively and remain frustrated. I listen to people regularly who describe an unsatisfactory experience and either they don't know how to complain, they aren't organized to make their case, they are too lazy to make time to complain or, worse yet, they have no case.

I usually ask them, why don't you write the company? And they answer somewhat evasively: I don't have time; it wouldn't do any good; who knows where to write; what's the point?

Sometimes, the organization is right and you're wrong. Live with it. Complaining for the sake of complaining is wrong. It happened to me every now and then. A student received his or her final course grade from me and complained about it. In my response, I would review my grading system, the student's class attendance, the student's test and term paper grades, and other measures and indicated to him or her why I assigned the grade I did. Typically, the student admitted that he or she knew there was no case for changing the grade; he or she just wanted to try to see if the professor would give away in response to the complaint what the student did not earn in the classroom. That's awful, absolutely awful.

Don't do that. **If you have no case, just keep quiet.** There is the old fable that even a fish wouldn't get into such trouble if it could keep its mouth shut. If you complain without cause, it is similar to the Aesop fable of the boy who cried wolf. Every complaint without basis makes it more difficult for those with a situation meriting resolution to gain the reasonable resolution they seek. Don't mess it up for others.

As a final comment in this introductory section, even when the facts suggest you are right, you can't always obtain satisfaction. Twice, many years apart, I had differences with two separate companies about furniture purchases. In the first case, the manager of a store of this historic American mass retailer agreed that I was absolutely right but offered me no satisfaction.

We had ordered furniture as the arrival date for our second child neared; the mass retailer – or, more accurately, its store in what then was Northglenn mall in Northglenn, Colorado, a suburb of Denver – didn't deliver it when promised [the reason the store offered wasn't clear] and agreed to postpone charging our company credit card until we received the furniture – a reasonable position to take. However, that promise aside, the company charged us finances charges on the postponed bill even as it deleted the charge for the furniture [again – we had not yet received the furniture but we were liable for finance charges on a postponed bill??], then late payment finance charges on the finance charges on the bill which after much complaining from me the company deleted and so on and so forth.

It took several months to clear up the situation and for us to receive the bedroom furniture. Worse yet, the store manager after I complained admitted the furniture had been in the warehouse the entire time. I suggested a resolution that seemed reasonable to me for both parties to resolve what the store manager agreed was his company's fault. [By the way, I thought it reasonable for me to pay the company's real, out-of-pocket cost for the bedroom furniture but not the mark-up to pay for store overhead, salaries, profit, etc. We had suffered and my suggestion would mean the company would cover its out-of-pocket costs but book no profit on the sale.

He declined; he offered nothing other than to clear up the credit account. I have never purchased again from that company, and given its sad financial state today – another major mass market retailer took it over several years ago after all – perhaps other customers had similarly unsatisfactory experiences and like me stayed away from the store chain.

In the second case, we had ordered a piece of furniture from a well-known furniture store in small town, central Iowa and I indicated that I worked at Iowa State University and I could literally be home to meet the delivery people in five minutes from the time they called from their previous delivery [Ames is a small city]. I asked and the salesperson agreed that the delivery folks would call me from their last stop in Ames and I would drive home and meet them to take delivery. Instead, the delivery men left the furniture – several end tables – which were badly scratched with our ten year old son – not satisfactory. How can one leave something of value with a minor child and have him sign for it? This repeated several times and finally I received the end tables without scratches and dents.

I wrote to complain. The company owner called me in response to my complaint letter in which I described what happened, including having a ten year old – a minor – sign for the delivery, agreed with me that I had a right to be upset, but declined my suggestion how to resolve the situation and ease my disappointment. Again, I never returned to that store. By the way, as in the case with the store in Colorado, I thought it reasonable that I pay the furniture store in Iowa enough money to cover the actual cash cost for the furniture and give me back the additional mark-up [for salaries, showroom costs, etc.] as a penalty for such poor customer service. Much as the Colorado store, the Iowa store owner apologized but refused to offer any financial concession to compensate for what he agreed was bad service; I have stayed away ever since.

Several years ago, a major newspaper in central Iowa, part of a larger national chain, as is so often the case today, announced as part of a larger company-wide policy change, that it was implementing a new pricing structure, whereby print subscribers whether they wanted or not would have to pay more for an online subscription. That is, beginning with this change, this newspaper would have only a two-tiered pricing system – online only or print and online but there was no print only [or third] alternative.

I wrote the local newspaper publisher, and she did not respond. I realized that she was implementing a policy that the corporate parent would soon implement for all its newspapers, so I wrote the CEO of the corporate parent and suddenly I received a call from the local publisher [amazing how that works!]; we talked for quite some time. I realize she was implementing a system-wide corporate office decision; but I wanted her to understand I had no interest in paying for the additional web access. We canceled our subscription, and so did a great many former subscribers to this highly-regarded paper in the heartland; in the end, I bet the corporate parent lost more money raising prices for unwanted web access than it gained from the increased price of the subscription. I view it as a loss for the newspaper chain – we halted our subscription – AND a loss for us – we halted our subscription. Perhaps new leadership at the corporate parent at some future time will realize the policy was mistaken and establish a three-tier policy.

In another situation, a larger, barbecue-style casual dining restaurant opened in our town; it was and remains a bit hit with central Iowans. We went one evening, and after dinner, I wrote the "contact us" address to make two suggestions about the menu. First, the menu featured pulled pork – and if it came from Iowa pigs it would be great pulled pork! – but no coleslaw. Seriously, how can one have pulled pork on a menu and not have coleslaw as a side? There was steamed broccoli but with pulled pork? And the apple pie dessert was clearly second rate, equal to the inexpensive pie one can purchase at a low price at a local grocery store.

I did not receive a response from the customer relations website, so I found the address for the corporate CEO and wrote him. As with the customer relations website, I did not receive any kind of response from the corporate president [who also was the founder]. In turn, I haven't returned to that restaurant neither its outlet in Ames nor anywhere else. I believe I made two reasonable suggestions and surely someone could take a moment if only to acknowledge my comment, thank me for it, and dismiss my suggestion all at the same time. But someone at the company should acknowledge every reasonable communication.

Let me contrast this non-response with the absolutely terrific response by a very popular grocery store chain that originated in Iowa although it has now expanded into surrounding states. For our wedding anniversary, I ordered a small, yellow marble cake with chocolate frosting and raspberry filling between the layers. I went to pick up the cake and it clearly was a white cake with white frosting. I paid for it and went home, and then decided I was annoyed. I wrote the "contact us" site for the grocery chain. Literally within ten minutes the store manager had called me, indicating he had received my message from the centralized corporate website [a lot of companies can learn from this!], he checked my order and I was right, and he said the bakery was frosting a new cake right then and he would bring it to our home [which he did with a container of ice cream]. This was exceptional and I quickly wrote the company to thank the person who handled the customer service web site **and** the local manager who obviously is destined for greater things within that corporation. And, to cap off this story, in December 2013, the grocery chain named the manager of this Ames grocery store as its store manager of the year; and some months later promoted him to regional manager for central Iowa. I would like to think that his concern for customers and their appreciation of that concern as evidenced by our exchange over the cakes played a huge part in earning that honor.

You cannot complain and if you do not receive a satisfactory resolution go back to frequenting that establishment. If you really are upset, and I really was upset, then you have to say that's it and end the business relationship. So it goes. If the organization receives enough complaints over poor service, if its leadership or perhaps its outside financiers wonder or worry about a decline in finances or sales, then you have made your point.

CHAPTER THREE

The Chinese Censorate

[This may seem like an aside but it really isn't.]

In the strongest Chinese dynasties going back hundreds and hundreds of years, there was an institution called the censorate. It functioned very differently from what you might imagine; it did not seek to prevent the free flow of information but rather the opposite. The emperor took officials out of the bureaucracy for a limited, term appointment; they had the obligation to travel the country and the right to report their findings directly to the emperor. In this fashion, the emperor – and strong emperors wanted this – would know if his government functioned effectively and if not he could resolve the issue before either it failed to serve the people or they become so disgusted that they revolted. Although the censorate reached back to the Qin Dynasty [221-206 BCE], by the time of the Ming Dynasty [1368-1644 CE], the six major "cabinet" departments established their own respective censorate operations.

By the way, after a fixed term, these officials, the censors, rotated back into the normal bureaucracy and if they had unfairly accused officials while in the Censorate, presumably they faced a kind of retribution on returning to the bureaucracy – a check on censorate excesses.

If you think about it, with a proper, detailed, reasonable complaint, you are functioning as the unpaid censorate for corporate and government America. These organizational heads should – and likely will - appreciate what you are doing because your complaint probably reflects bigger problems that could threaten the smooth functioning of the organization and its ability to deliver the services or products and earn the profits for which it exists.

And good CEOs want their organization to function smoothly and to serve its various publics, customers, and end users well. If such good CEOs don't hear from customers directly, they have to rely on subordinates who also may not have access to what is happening at the retail sites be they physical - a store - or electronic - the Internet. You are helping them improve their organization and every good CEO is committed to improving his or her organization.

For this reason, I disagree with some web sites I have seen where the web site creator, offering good and useful information, recommends writing the "customer relations" site and explicitly not writing the corporate or organizational CEO. These sites note that no CEO likely will ever see your letter and you will obtain better results in writing to customer relations. They correctly note that CEOs are very busy individuals, and have little time to spare, which is absolutely true. And, depending on the kind of letter you write, they could be correct. But, if you write politely, in detail, and with a positive purpose, I believe you will be pleasantly surprised by the response you will receive.

I want to emphasize in writing you are not trying to get something out of the company or organization; you want to help it improve its processes. Ann and I like to drive every several months to the Twin Cities for the weekend, visit Mall of America, tour a museum or the zoo, have a nice dinner, see something the next morning and return home that afternoon. On one trip, we went to one of the fast, casual restaurant outlets in the mall. I received my burrito quickly and efficiently; not so with Ann. The restaurant was out of grilled chicken and apparently with some haste the grill man threw perhaps twenty marinated chicken breasts on the heat. To me, there had to be an expeditor, someone responsible for the smooth running of the operation and he or she had failed to keep on top of the supply of grilled chicken.

I wrote the national office for this fast casual restaurant chain that evening. I liked the reply. Someone in the main office responded to me with a nice, e-mailed note of apology and, more importantly, copied perhaps a dozen people working for the company, presumably someone at that particular restaurant, perhaps someone in charge of training expeditors, perhaps a regional manager, etc. I didn't recognize the names, but the e-mails all ended with the company's e-mail extension. She recognized a potential problem in what should be a smooth running operation and moved to improve it. It was a good reaction to my e-mail; this restaurant chain is a good company with good food and a commitment, at least by the response I received, to serving its customers.

Sometimes you have to persist if you feel strongly about what occurred. We flew on one of America's large airlines to visit my mom in south Florida in January 2013; we were returning through its major hub when the situation occurred. We were supposed to board a flight from that hub back to Des Moines and return home by late afternoon. Instead, there was a flight delay, and another delay and another delay, ten minutes here, twenty minutes there. The gate agents had no information and did not seem particularly interested in securing any to share with the increasingly upset passengers wishing to fly to Des Moines. And we were told the flight could leave any minute so we could not leave the gate area for example, to buy a meal. Worse yet, at that time, the food court on that concourse at that airport was closed so we could not leave to find food elsewhere or risk the plane leaving.

In the end the flight was delayed four hours and, to add insult to injury, as we were boarding the plane and only as we were boarding the plane, a gate agent handed out food coupons which we could not use at that hub for reasons noted above and there was no time anyways because we had to board the plane immediately they kept telling us]; we could not use them in Des Moines because by the time this delayed flight would land, food service in Des Moines would have closed for the night. By the way, the cabin crew on the regional carrier were warm and friendly and did a great job. But I thought that the large airline's hub Atlanta station manager [however titled] should have acted quickly to do something for the passengers on this long-delayed flight.

Separately, I was returning from Detroit and a weeklong research trip to the Gerald Ford Library in Ann Arbor to Des Moines five months later. While waiting for the return flight that evening, I noticed the flight across the concourse from our flight had been delayed. By way of contrast, the company's Detroit airport operations brought a flatbed of bottled water and juices and snacks for those passengers and while the gate agents regularly provided updates so at least passengers were informed of the situation. That was a good job. The mess at the hub airport on the return from Florida was a failure of management in that airline's operations in Atlanta while the well-handled situation in Detroit, the delayed flight aside, was to the credit of the station manager who worked for the same company.

So, I wrote this major American carrier to complain. I wrote the "contact us" address initially and received little satisfaction. I began writing the CEO. If we had been bumped to another flight leaving four hours later, a US airline would have offered some significant compensation, likely several hundred dollars in credit towards a future flight; and the utter lack of information and what most of us took to be the insult with the unusable food coupon bothered me. It took several letters, explaining and re-explaining how I thought the airline had failed, to secure the reaction I wanted. If it bothers you enough, persist! And I still fly that airline; the CEO's office responded and that response deserves my business.

Sometimes, you don't win but you don't lose. We have our insurance – property and automobile – with a wonderful national company. However, once a year for some years we received an unsigned letter, unless you count the corporate "name" as a name and signature – there was no person signing the letter, e.g., Charles Dobbs, Vice President, the company, informing us that the insurer had hired an outside survey firm to contact those policyholders who received the letter to ask questions about automobile usage. I always assumed the company had some metrics for typical usage and if one fell outside so many standard deviations of that typical profile – bingo, you received the letter. We live in a college town; eight months of the year, there are 62,000 residents; four months a year – when most students are gone, the town drops down to about 30,000. I would always describe the size of town to note why we don't drive that many miles – it just isn't that far to get from here to there in our community. Most of the interviewers for this outside survey firm live in major metropolitan areas with populations in the millions - how could they understand what it is like driving in a small city?

And, more than half the times, the company wound up reducing our six month premium by a negligible amount, the most recent time, by $1.69 for six months [for two cars]. Isn't this a waste of time and don't the company's clients deserve better information about the reasons for the process and their selection?

In December 2013, I decided I was bothered by the letter. I wrote the insurance company CEO to complain. Apparently, the CEO, to his credit, reviews a certain number of customer letters regularly; ours made it to his desk. I have since received several telephone calls from staff but no resolution. The staffer agreed I had a point, but would not commit to my suggestion of forwarding the company letter, my letter, and my proposed revisions to the responsible corporate officer and suggest a major edit.

Oh well. If I worked for this insurance/finance company CEO, I would have drafted a letter to me noting I had a good idea about having a name and title noted as the originator of the letter and not just the corporate acronym; I would further have noted that we were referring my letter to the "underwriting division" to add that name; second, I would have said we would ask staff in that division to play with wording of the letter that, without giving away corporate secrets, would explain the reasons generally for the survey information demand and why the company seemingly regularly selects some clients to survey and not others.

This last one may seem silly, but I admit I am bothered. I write presidents of the United States at the www.whitehouse.gov web address on matters of foreign relations; I am a diplomatic historian and it's my field of expertise. President George W. Bush and President Barack Obama each provided a place to offer a comment or suggestion or criticism and the site had a box one may check if one wants to receive a response. I have always checked that box; I have never received a response. Perhaps I need to be more effective, as most likely so do you!

By the way, the result seems to be that I regularly receive e-mails from various Democratic Party-affiliated groups and print mails from various Republican Party-affiliated groups. [The different communication styles are interesting!] That is, the separate, successive White House organizations assume senders of e-mails are faithful party members reflecting the party of the sitting president. A shame, because I write good letters reflecting my professional life as a diplomatic historian.

CHAPTER FOUR
Gathering your Facts

You need to get your facts straight. I remember many letters and some telephone calls from parents complaining about a child's experience at the institutions at which I worked. When I looked into the situation, I almost always found the child had lied - or certainly misstated the facts - to his or her parents and, in one sad case, to his grandparents. The parents, trusting their respective child and wanting to help, complained honestly but in ignorance.

I often felt badly for the parents [and the grandparents] but rarely for the child, the student at my institution. In one case, a parent repeated a child's claim that a professor in a large lecture class had it in for him and that accounted for the bad grade that failed him out of school. To "earn" a GPA less than 2.0 takes work, and that means less than satisfactory work in more than one class and over more than one semester. That is, one has to regularly miss classes and regularly fail to turn in assignments over a long period of time. In the meantime how does one pass his or her time when one's roommates, friends, and classmates are all walking off to class?

I taught large lecture classes; so I wondered what must this student be doing during class to receive the professor's attention? How disruptive was he? For the most part, it is hard to remember many students from such large classes; if he allegedly made such a strong and negative impression, what the heck was he doing?

Sometimes I used a bit of a subterfuge in responding. I wrote the parents – in one heartbreaking case, the grandparents, who literally re-mortgaged the farm to help a favored grandchild go to college and that grandchild just goofed off, failed to attend class, flunked out, took their hard-earned funds, and felt no guilt about it – indicating that the facts were not quite what they had described but, because of student privacy rights, I could not explain it all to them. I then wrote the student about whom the parents complained at his or her "permanent" – that is, home – rather than campus or temporary address and explained everything. I sent both letters home - to the same address. More than once, a parent opened both letters, including the one properly addressed to their child, and realized what the truth of the situation. One time I received a reply from a grateful parent that she and her husband had a "come to Jesus" meeting with the child and to me that was a good outcome.

You need to begin by gathering facts for your argument. This could include receipts, advertisements, or copy information from the packaging. It could be writing out a time sequence to put events into context. It could be a statement indicating your expertise or knowledge. It could be your memory of events fully written out. It could be notes you took at the time or that you wrote as soon as possible after you finished speaking with a company representative or the customer relations department. Such notes are particularly critical if you are claiming that a company, store or organizational employee promised you something, and you need to state very carefully that promise and why you want it honored. I sometimes "zone out" during meetings – I doodle by playing out famous chess games and drawing various positions, e.g., Robert Fischer's "game of the century" again Robert Byrne at the 1963-64 US Closed Championship – and so early in my professional career I developed the habit of taking extensive meeting notes if only to remain in the conversation. That was great practice for taking notes and/or reconstructing conversations after the fact. Consider practicing note taking; you remember the old joke: "How do you get to Carnegie Hall? Practice, practice, practice! What proof do you have that some company or organization did not live up to promises made?

You need to realize that, if the person to whom you address your letter thinks you have a case, he or she will have someone look into the issues you raised. There better be substance to back up your issues. Details always help. And you need to be accurate.

Let me give you two examples of the utter need to have your facts accurate. Some years ago in the president's office at ISU an irate woman called to complain, at length, about a course the university was offering. She thought the course immoral and that we, the university, and certainly the president should be ashamed. As I was speaking with her generally about the meaning of "academic freedom" - that faculty members in their areas of expertise had the right to pursue any line of inquiry and to report on that because the risk of limiting that freedom was greater than its occasional abuse, I was looking up the supposed course. I couldn't find it. Perhaps, on a whim, I checked the semester course schedule for another highly-regarded public university in Iowa, the University of Iowa. Sure enough, the semester schedule listed the course about which she was complaining. I finished my defense because it is worth defending the principle of academic freedom, and explained she had the wrong university. Couldn't we do something about that course? No, absolutely not.

Similarly, years before that, at Metro State, an irate caller complained about a religious studies course a faculty member supposedly was teaching. I discussed academic freedom generally and the differences between a religion department, which public universities do not have, and a religious studies department, which many public universities do have. Again, as I was speaking with the caller, I checked our semester schedule - no such course. Again, on a whim, I checked the semester schedule at the University of Colorado at Denver - the state of Colorado set up a strange system where three separate institutions of higher education - Metro State, UCD, and the Community College of Denver - all reporting to separate governing boards occupied common space which a fourth state agency, a landlord, the Auraria Higher Education Center, oversaw. It was in many ways a confusing and likely inefficient arrangement. As with the previous case, I told the caller she needed to contact the proper, which in this case was, the UCD administration.

Get your facts straight. You look silly calling the wrong organization or company and you waste time - your own and whoever takes your call.

You need to be clear when you write to complain. However, don't be overly dramatic, keep value judgment comments to a minimum. Like Jack Webb on the old TV show, *Dragnet,* "just the facts." Don't write it was the worst experience of your life if it wasn't or that you'll never recover unless you truly will never recover. Be calm, be reasonable, and be firm. Avoid histrionics. Employees who review complaints do so very often; write clearly, politely, accurately, and firmly and they will realize there is something different, compelling about your letter compared to others that go to complaint departments or CEO offices.

And, related to avoiding histrionics, fit the emotion to the situation. My wife, Ann, likes the skim milk, low calorie vanilla ice cream sandwiches that a particular company sells. It is her favorite weekday after-dinner treat especially during warmer weather months. One evening, she opened a package and noticed that half of the chocolate cookie in one side was missing. I suggested she e-mail the company and she gave me her "look."

So I e-mailed the company! I noted the situation, where we bought the product, the identifying numbers, and in a separate paragraph I wrote that I like watching the "Food Factory" and other, similar programs on television. I am always fascinated to see the laser lights and other equipment that measures and evaluates every product as it moves down the production line and knocks away, often with a puff of air, products that do not meet the particular company's standard. And I expressed my wonderment that such did not happen at this company's dairy plant. I didn't write angrily; I didn't state we'd never buy the product again; I just pointed out a fault in that one ice cream sandwich and wondered what had gone wrong at the dairy plant.

I received a prompt and very nice response from a company representative and several days later a coupon in the mail for a free package of the ice cream sandwiches. Ann has already eaten that package and we've bought many more in the months since the incident. She feels better, and this company has cemented a relationship with one customer who tells colleagues and friends about the wonderful customer service response. **Remember, write in moderation.**

An example: many, many years ago – when I was still in graduate school – I had purchased a popular brand of granola cereal; there was a cookie recipe on the box; the company indicated it would be one of the best cookies one ever made [and ate]. Well, I made the cookies and they were adequate but not great; the cereal, a very good granola cereal, however still is terrific. I wrote a letter to the corporate kitchens just to indicate my reaction. And since this was more than 30 years ago when more women cooked at home than men especially with married couples, I also indicated my background as the daily cook and principal baker in our household. The issue was the recipe, to me, not what the corporate kitchens might presume incorrectly as my relative inexperience as a home cook.

I had a nice exchange with the head of the corporate kitchen and I was satisfied. She refunded the purchase price of the granola cereal which I still very much like to eat, although, being much older, I eat the low fat variety now. And I haven't made those cookies again!

CHAPTER FIVE

Organizing your Argument

As with millions and millions of Americans, we have a cell phone plan. I know, whoopee. We got to the point where the phones we owned were more than a few years old, and we thought about getting new ones. Interestingly, when we received the next monthly bill for service, the cell phone company had an insert more or less telling us [and millions of other customers] if we visited a company-owned store on a certain upcoming Saturday in early fall 2012, we could obtain a new cell phone for free.

Such a deal ☺.

We went to a company-owned store in a large mall in West Des Moines, Iowa and learned the company intended the free phones only for the most expensive cell phone plan which we did not have nor wanted. However, a store salesperson indicated that less expensive, perhaps more entry level phones we wanted had a big rebate and he would help us fill out and submit the rebate form for us. Terrific. We thanked him a lot.

As luck would have it, several months later, we received notice from the company that we did not qualify for the rebate. It wasn't the money. I was annoyed that a company employee told us about the rebate, filled out the form for us, and arranged to submit it. The company had to honor the actions of its employee.

When I was in president's offices I always believed if a complainant had reasonable cause to believe that a university employee should have known the rules, I felt we had to side with the complainant. If we did not properly train the employee, even if the complainant was wrong, it was our problem. Of course, if I found the same employee or same office regularly made the same error again and again, I took care of that [I met with that office's superior and discussed the complaints with a suggestion about a course of action to follow]. We didn't have to agree our policy or procedure was at fault, but we couldn't hold the student responsible for following advice of an employee who should have known better.

I found the corporate address for the cell phone company. I described the advertisement we received, the visit to the company-owned store, our purchase, the employee filling out the forms and consulting with the store manager. I recounted my approach as assistant to the president noted above and why I thought the cell phone company had to honor the rebate form.

I received a telephone call a week later from the executive office and an assistant to the CEO told me we would receive our rebate, which we did. The phone call and the action offered showed this was a good company ... hats off to them! We stay with companies that honor their promises and we have stayed with that particular cell phone company.

In another situation, my sister, Debbie, and I planned a 90th birthday celebration for our mother. I purchased plane tickets for my wife and me to fly from Des Moines to LaGuardia Airport in New York City and then to rent a car to drive to Connecticut for the family gathering. We used a major internet travel company and its web site. Several weeks after we purchased the tickets, I received an e-mail from the travel company indicating the airline we would use for the return leg of the flight was leaving the Des Moines market and I needed to call the travel company to arrange for rebooking on another airline.

The agent on the telephone insisted we could only rebook on one airline, not either of the airlines we had originally chosen, and that we had to travel from LaGuardia Airport in New York City through Dallas several hours out of the way rather than through Chicago which was a straight shot flying over I-80 from New York City through Chicago to Des Moines. This was not a comment on the airline company; it was a comment on the travel company representative telling us we had no choice on airline or flight and connecting hub.

This made no sense, and I decided to complain. The airline in question gained nothing from flying us so far off course; it could fly us more directly. A representative of this company told me that I had to contact the airline that was leaving the Des Moines market to secure its permission to arrange for the flights I wanted on another airline and on a more direct routing, e.g., from LaGuardia through Chicago or Detroit. A representative for the airline I wanted to use gave me another story, that I had to call the airline we wanted to use to return from New York City, and so on and so forth until I was told I had no choice but to book an airline and fly from Des Moines to Dallas-Fort Worth airport to LaGuardia – rather roundabout and a waste of several hours.

It seemed ridiculous to me but I could not break this cycle where I had to talk to the travel company and then the first airline and so on. No one wanted to take responsibility for booking the flights we wanted although no one opposed us wanting those flights.

I wrote the CEO of the travel company and soon received an e-mail asking me to call a certain person in the customer service office who offered to book us on the substitute flights we wanted – from Des Moines to Chicago to LaGuardia or straight down I-80 from west to east and back! I wrote a "thank you" note to this internet travel company for agreeing to correct the booking. We patronize companies that serve their customers.

One day I purchased a package of frozen pulled pork barbecue at a discount warehouse in Ames. Living in Iowa, we had the country's best pork and I liked to purchase half of a Boston butt and make my own - low and slow. But I was lazy that day and I thought, well, someone had already done the work for me, and, after, it was pulled pork barbecue - how could one go wrong. It was wrong or at least not for us. There was an overwhelming black pepper taste and little else - not cumin, chili pepper, herbs,

49

paprika, garlic, onions or the signature ingredient of the company selling the product.

I was disappointed and I wrote a brief note to the company that made the pork barbecue. I quickly received a nice note and a check to refund my purchase [I had supplied the receipt, location, date, etc. in my original letter]. I appreciated the response and I hope the company rethinks its spice blend for the frozen pulled pork.

In April 1977 we bought a new car, our first such purchase, in anticipation of both of us finishing graduate school and securing jobs in our respective fields – we were so naïve! By the late 1980s the fenders had faded, no longer silver but really just a dull gray with some rust [I always blamed the eruption of Mount St. Helens and the resulting ash cloud]. I was at the dealership located but a few blocks from our former house in Northglenn, Colorado one day for servicing - an oil change I think. I happened to ask the service manager how come the automobile manufacturer didn't have to replace the front fenders given the fading. He responded there had been a recall and I failed to respond.

I asked how the company informed car owners and somewhat serendipitously a regional rep for the company happened to be in the dealership that day. He said the company sent postcards to all its car owners, and I replied why wouldn't I have brought my car the several blocks from my house to replace the fenders? He responded that, if I could prove I was in a dealership between that day and some three months earlier, the window of time in which to respond to the free fender replacement offer, he would authorize [as in the company would pay the dealership] for my new fenders.

I walked home, grabbed our receipt folder for that year, and returned to the dealership. Once a year I purchase a folder with monthly slots and we throw receipts in by the month; I only had to thumb through three months of receipts and within a few minutes I found a receipt. Bingo - free replacement fenders. Keep good and organized records; it can pay off for you.

Sometimes it doesn't work out. Here's yet another example. In 1991, we purchased a new car to replace that 1977 purchase, and it was a good purchase. The car delivered what it was supposed to deliver for many years. Ten years later the automatic seat belts – some cars of that era had automatically closing and retracting shoulder – but not lap - belts rather than air bags to meet National Highway Transportation Safety Board passive restraint requirements - failed. I thought and I still believe that the automobile manufacturer should have guaranteed or been required to guarantee those passive restraints for the life of the car; the dealership disagreed; I wrote the manufacturer's customer service office and it disagreed; the company's route person on a visit to the dealership disagreed. So, we owned bought that one car from the company and won't buy another - silly for the manufacturer, silly for us.

CHAPTER SIX

Writing the letter

There are steps in writing the letter. Consider formatting the letter appropriately. A letter that looks nice and is nicely spaced on the page will help present your argument in a better light. You also want to select a readable font; don't select one too strange – it may be difficult to read on the page. Don't select one too small to save a piece of paper; perhaps the CEO can't read such small print; don't select a font or a font size too large simply to make your letter seem longer. If you don't have much experience in formatting a letter, most word processing programs have such a function and have examples of formatting. And if your printer's ink cartridge is running dry, replace it before printing the letter and/or envelope.

The very first meeting of my graduate research methods class at Indiana University back in the mid-1970s, the professor, Robert H. Ferrell, who subsequently became my dissertation chair, came into the room and began by passing around toothpicks to each of us. After each of us had taken the five he said we should take, he then spoke his first words – "go to your apartment and clean your typewriter keys; I want clean copy – not just free of typographical and grammatical errors, I want those letters that are gummed up to strike cleanly." In the old days of manual typewriters, many typewriter ribbons were fabric, and well-used letters/keys would become clogged – "e's", "s's", and "t's" especially.

He was right; so in a more modern sense, follow his advice and replace the printer ink cartridge if need be, use white paper, format the page and take pride in your writing. The more thoughtful your presentation, the better impression your letter will make, and the more satisfactory a response you'll receive.

Professor Ferrell used to emphasize the importance of the opening to one's dissertation or research paper. He thought the opening had to help the reader settle into his or her chair and interest them in continuing to read further. Ditto for your letter. Even if the company or organization has a web site and you wish to complain in the box or area where it encourages you to write, consider writing first in your word processor, edit it, check spelling and grammar, and then cut and paste your complaint into this complaint "box." As the TV commercial for a certain under arm deodorant used to go, "you never get a second chance to make a first impression."

Also letters should have rhythm. An English department colleague at my first institution, Eugene Saxe, charted out several Shakespearean plays, word-by-word, an amazingly time intensive effort but the results were worth that prodigious effort. He showed that Shakespeare's first and last acts tended to be the shortest and with the most monosyllabic words and the shortest sentences. The middle acts – think *Hamlet* – were longer, more complex and had those memorable soliloquies. That is, Shakespeare wasn't just a brilliant playwright, he also mastered basic writing and organization that allowed him to write so powerfully.

Keep that in mind while writing your complaint letter. Generally, you want a brief opening, a brief closing and several, most likely no more than three, solid, fact laden paragraphs. Keep letters under two pages; a page-and-a-half letter is a good length – long enough to make your point but not so long to require more time than the CEO you hope is reading your letter has time to read.

And if the situation really matters to you, as it should, take time to proofread your letter. You may wish to activate "Readability Statistics" in your word processing program. It not only checks spelling and grammar, it also gives you a snapshot of your writing clarity, complexity, etc. If you are interested, type "readability statistics" and the version of Microsoft's Word that you are using, e.g., "readability statistics in Word 2010" in your favorite online search engine. Follow the resulting directions.

Once you have turned on this feature and do a spelling/grammar review, you will receive information on the complexity or simplicity of your writing style, its ponderousness or clarity, and suggestions to improve that prose. A well-written letter of complaint is more convincing than a poorly composed one; it makes a good impression, and you want to make that good impression. It suggests you are serious, composed your letter thoughtfully, and thus your letter merits a serious reply.

I use this function because I have a tendency to write long paragraphs and, sometimes, long sentences. I was contributing a chapter to a friend's edited book several years ago and he commented how, in a 20 page article, I had perhaps a dozen paragraphs. I took the hint and went back and broke down the overly long paragraphs – several were more than 3 and 4 pages long – into something more readable. Do the same if your writing has easily corrected flaws.

I guess I am a student of Robert Ferrell, for I require all students whether in the undergraduate or graduate research methods classes to turn on Readability Statistics and to be aware of their writing, sentence structure, etc. One graduate student in another department whose committee recommended she take my research methods classes to strengthen her writing became so engrossed in this function that she would stop virtually every sentence to check her statistics. That's too much, but one wants to make a good impression whether it is via a print letter, an e-mail, a telephone call or a face-to-face conversation.

First, gather your facts. What happened? When? Where? Why didn't it go as you wanted? Did you complain immediately to someone on-site or perhaps immediately to someone over the telephone? What was the response? What did you expect, and why were you disappointed with the response from this first level of review. The more details within reason [there is no need to describe the weather unless the weather mattered to the complaint] the better. Construct a time line for the event in question including the time line of your complaining up to the point of contacting the organizational CEO and, if need be, have documentation to attach to the complaint.

THE INITIAL LETTER

Let's begin with the initial letter, sometimes a complaint, sometimes an inquiry, and sometimes just an information item. At this point, while some product, some action, some event may have disappointed you, you are now approaching the company or organization for the first time seeking redress.

Approach with an optimistic outlook for, in the overwhelming majority of cases, your initial letter will be successful. You were right to complain; the company wants to make good and to have satisfied customers; and everything works out. Terrific!

Still, you need to organize thoughts, gather information, and explain yourself. In this initial letter, keep it brief. Sometimes, by the way, it isn't even a letter; you just walk up to the customer service desk or ask for the manager and receive whatever you were seeking. An example: several years ago our microwave oven died; it happens. I went to one of America's largest discount stores to purchase a new one. When I got home and we took the microwave out of the box and plugged it in, nothing happened. I read through the instruction booklet, looked for any switch, button or anything to push, pull or turn and still no luck. I called our local store on the telephone and customer service told me to bring it right back. A few minutes later I had a new microwave which still works just fine.

In another instance, some years ago an income tax preparation software company offered a $10.00 rebate on the purchase of its particular and well-regarded software which along with millions of other Americans, we use to fill out tax returns and pay our taxes. I filled out the form, mailed it, the UPC code, and the receipt to the specified address, but not before making a photocopy of everything. Weeks went by, and I didn't receive my $10.00 rebate. I e-mailed the company and attached a scanned copy of the packet and soon thereafter the company's customer service operation mailed me a coupon good on the next year's purchase which I used because we still use that firm's tax preparation software. It only took a simple inquiry and proof we had complied with the rebate rules.

On a very different vein, I really like the Baker Chocolate four square brownie recipe which for years was on the Baker unsweetened chocolate package [with the blocks of chocolate inside]. Well, stupid me, I never cut out or wrote out the recipe because I always assumed it would be on the package. Then it wasn't - there was a new, lighter, two square recipe. I wrote the corporate kitchens and a very nice food technician wrote back - actually typed for it was that long ago - the old recipe. I still have the page she typed and sent me. Today I realize one likely can go on-line and search the Internet for this sort of thing but one can also make a simple inquiry to the company.

I have also written companies about products I liked that local stores did not have just to ask if it was a space issue - the company wanted to market [if it were the producer] or to stock [if it were the end seller] other goods - or did declining sales result in a decision to discontinue. For example, I own seven dark blue men's dress shirts from one particular company; obviously I like them. I also own a few dark blue dress shirts from several other companies. Then the main company seemingly stopped selling them in its stores; so I wrote; I received my reply. I will have to live with it.

On the other hand, more than twenty five years ago, an enterprising fellow, a student at the University of Tennessee, Paul Hethmon, decided he wanted to press the Mars Candy Company to bring back the red M&M. Mars from 1976 to 1985 had stopped producing red M&Ms out of fear about Red Dye #2 but Mars used other red dyes - no real problem. And they were red M&Ms! *The Wall Street Journal* had an article describing this fellow's mission; if people would send him $10.00, he would sign them up for his Society for the Restoration and Preservation of Red M&Ms and send them form postcards they in turn could send to the Mars people to ask them to bring back the red M&M. Silly, yes; but effective? Absolutely! I was one of thousands I am sure he signed up for the campaign. Not long after the column appeared in the *WSJ,* and presumably after these thousands signed up and sent off their petitions, Mars brought back the red M&M. A great day for the consumer!

And in a silly case, when I received my Ph.D. degree many years ago, my favorite three aunts bought me a navy blue soft-sided attaché case from a terrific company which I used every work day to haul around notes, tests, and more recently laptop computers. And, after three-and-a-half decades of great service, it began to tear. Quelle dommage! I bought a new one and within a few weeks I somehow lost one of the little leather pieces which one used to pull the various zippers open and shut. I wrote the company's customer service operation and people there nicely mailed me several replacement pieces. That easy interaction is one reason we have been loyal customers for many decades.

WRITING THE MORE SERIOUS LETTER
OR FOLLOW-UP LETTER

With your information at your fingertips, let's begin writing the more serious letter or, perhaps, the follow-up to a lower-key letter that did not result in the outcome you wanted. The first paragraph has to be brief: you are disappointed [or even "very upset"] over a situation that occurred on such-and-such date either at the store located wherever or the organization office or through the Internet. Someone will open your letter and a brief, clear opening paragraph will help move your letter to someone in authority who can, if you are correct, rectify your situation.

Here's an example:

I am writing to express my disappointment with your company. On August 8, I purchased this item and the store would not honor the sale price in the advertisement. I hope you will review the situation and agree that I deserve the additional discount and you will credit our charge account.

Assuming you enclosed a copy of the advertisement and your receipt, the CEO or his/her assistant can easily assign this to someone who can rectify the situation.

Or:

Your company advertised a rebate for the purchase of certain items over the Memorial Day weekend. We purchased a new vacuum cleaner, enclosed the proper documentation, and received a response several weeks later that the rebate was denied.

This is not exactly on point, but over the years I have read a great many job application letters for faculty and administrative openings. Perhaps one in ten letters failed to mention the position for which the applicant was applying. Imagine the fate of that application, especially if the office receiving such applications has more than one job opening or if one is applying through the institution's human resources unit for routing applications to appropriate academic departments! But it does make it easier on the search committee – no need to waste time on something destined for the proverbial circular file.

Similarly, at least one in ten job applicants did not meet the minimum qualifications for the position. In a search for a historian of China, for example, some historians with other specialties will apply – it is a tight job market. Again, it just makes the job of the search committee easier. Or they lack the required background, degree, etc. Be sure your situation merits attention from senior organizational leaders. You want your situation or the way in which the company handled your situation to compel action from the CEO's office.

One more example:

On Thursday evening last week, my wife and I dined at your restaurant in Bloomington, Minnesota [the town doesn't matter for the example]. We were discouraged in general by the restaurant's appearance which seemed dirty and the lackadaisical attitude of the wait staff. However I am writing to tell you about our reaction to the food we received.

Yet another example:

Dear Provost Allen: I acknowledge receipt of your recent letter informing me that the University will rescind my graduation unless I arrange for the course instructor to submit the grade for the summer course I took. I am writing to protest in the strongest possible manner the effort of the University to make the student responsible for the course instructor submitting grades when that is a function of the department chair, dean, and yourself.

The second paragraph is chock full of details. Here's what happened; here's why I am upset; here's how I tried to resolve the situation informally or at a lower level; and here's why I failed [obviously because the organization or company isn't responsive at this lower level].

Let's follow the first letter:

I am enclosing a copy of your company's national advertisement clearly noting the additional sale – 30% off – on top of the existing sale price. The ad mentioned no exclusions. I am also enclosing a copy of our receipt showing that we purchased the item within the sale period. Finally, I am attaching a clean copy of my rough typed notes of the unsatisfactory telephone conversation I had with the store manager after I returned home.

Here's another example:

We used your Internet travel site to purchase airplane tickets for a family event. As our travel date approached, I received an urgent e-mail message informing me I had to call one of your company's toll-free telephone numbers. When I called I learned our flights had been cancelled [the airline was pulling out of the Des Moines market] and your representative insisted we had to accept a not very direct routing when we had purchased such a direct routing and additional such routings existed. I protested and he insisted we had to follow this roundabout routing.

A few days later I decided I was sufficiently upset and wanted to complain. When I called the airline, a different representative indicated we could have requested the more direct routing but now we would have to pay a change-of-routing fee of $150.00. This is not acceptable. I called your *service number and the agent could not help me. Why would I voluntarily request a routing that was hours longer than what I had originally booked? I believe the problem rests within your firm, and I hope you will correct this situation.*

Back to the letter to the provost:

I attended that course every day; I earned an "A" grade which was not surprising since my overall GPA was in excess of 3.8. How did the instructor leave town for a late summer vacation without turning in the grade? How did the department chair fulfill his summer duties without checking that every summer teaching faculty submitted grades in timely fashion? How did all the staff who support the work of the college dean allow this to take place? And how can you possibly hold the student – me – accountable for this administrative error?

Remember, the keys are details and clearly focusing on the event or sequence and not the people. If you attack employees, some CEOs will feel obligated to defend their good people and that's not a bad thing. Stick to the events, suggest it is not what you expected of such an organization, and you want satisfaction.

The third [or, perhaps, the fourth] paragraph should detail what you expected to happen or the resolution to the problem you sought from that first line supervisor. In both of these paragraphs be polite. Don't attack the people with whom you interacted. No nasty language and certainly no threats.

Again, an example:

Since your employee booked us on this round-about routing, and since he could have booked on us a more direct routing which I requested, I want your company to change our booking to replicate the routing which we originally had booked.

Politeness does not mean obfuscation. Be clear. A real example of mine: I wrote the CEO of an Iowa-based grocery store chain. The chain opened a new store near to our house. Several Saturday mornings in a row when I returned home from shopping, I found the bananas at the bottom of my paper sack, already bruising, and so no one would want to eat them. In my letter, I noted how I asked the cashier and the young sacker [a different person each week] to please put the bananas atop the sack and, indeed, any fruit or anything that was soft [e.g., a package of fresh mushrooms]. And I noted sadly that they didn't do it. I wondered in my letter about what kind of training the student hourly employees received, and I suggested a brief training session since my first regular job as a 16 year old was as a grocery sacker and then as a cashier at a local grocery chain that no longer exists in Stamford, Connecticut.

The next time I visited the grocery I met the store manager [who was waiting to speak with me]; he indicated the training session they had for all cashiers and sackers, and that he was sorry for what happened. I like that grocery, particularly its butcher/meat area, the manager is very good and friendly, and I shopped there every week until we moved from Ames to Bloomington, Indiana where sadly that grocery chain does not have operations.

Dear President XXXX:

I used to shop at your downtown store in "everytown" every Saturday morning, although recently when you all opened the store in north "everytown" I switched from the downtown store to the new north one which is closer to our home.

I am writing because, for several weeks running, the sacker filled my paper sack somewhat willy-nilly where bananas and other soft fruit wound up on the bottom of the bag and had bruised before I got home to empty the sack.

Isn't there some kind of minimal training for sackers – cans, firm boxes, glass enclosed products on bottom, perhaps a layer of paper, e.g., paper towels or a box of tissues, next and finally soft products, especially fresh fruit and vegetables on top where they can't easily bruise?

As in this example with this terrific Iowa grocery chain and the earlier example about the terrific producer of low calorie ice cream sandwiches, this paragraph can be a suggestion to improve operations, not to ask for something. Sometimes you may complain because you are seeking a resolution; sometimes you complain because you genuinely think the company or organization needs to improve its operations, e.g., sacking bananas at the bottom.

In the next paragraph indicate why you feel the CEO you are writing should agree with you. Always be clear. If you are so fortunate that the head of the organization or a senior assistant reads your letter, you have but one chance to convince them to agree with your analysis of the situation and grant the outcome you badly want.

Back to the cellphone rebate letter:

Personnel in your company's store – not a third party operation – in Valley West Mall in West Des Moines told us about the rebate and filled out the form; they told us where to mail the form and the receipt. They were very clear that we qualified for the rebate on the purchase of the new telephones. If the rebate process was so complicated that we did not qualify, then there was something wrong with the rebate offer itself.

Here is another example of the end of a letter:

Your bank holding company has a 100% satisfaction guarantee, and I am sure you will agree that, as a long time checking account holder with the bank and as one with a debit card, I have every right to expect that, when the bank switched its debit cards from MasterCard to Visa, it would have cleared the various ATM systems in the country. Put differently, I should have been able to use the ATM machine in a major regional bank branch in Indiana as well as using it in one of your bank branches in Iowa. Otherwise, what is the point?

And, when I called the toll-free customer service number on the debit card while on vacation and wanting additional cash and asked the customer service representative how could I access cash in our account while I was visiting family in Bloomington, Indiana, I deserved a better response than telling me that I should drive to a place where the bank had a branch, the nearest branch being more than two hours away.

By the way, the CEO sent a nice letter of explanation indicating the computer language glitch which he admitted was the bank's fault, apologized for the customer service representative's reply that we should drive two hours to another ATM machine, the CIO wrote similarly with a more detailed explanation of glitch in the switch from one system to another, and the bank honored its 100% guarantee by depositing $25.00 to our checking account; we stayed with that large banking company for nearly 20 years now. It was never the money; it was about complaining and hoping the bank system would improve the training of its customer service representatives. Apparently, I could have walked into any bank, handed over my debit card, and perhaps with a fee, obtained cash from our checking account. The rep should have known this and told me and that didn't happen.

And, last but certainly not least, indicate your appreciation for the CEO's time and attention. Your grandmother was right – always say "please" and "thank you." And mean it when you write it.

I appreciate your time and consideration and hope to hear from your office soon. I was disappointed with the situation I described and I have written to bring it to your attention.

CHAPTER SEVEN
Real World Complaint Letters

Again, you have proper name, title and address information; if you had problems securing this information, visit your local public library [or university library] and meet with an information services specialist. I am absolutely positive that such a trained professional can help you find the information you need.

Although you do have to pay for a stamp, send a written letter rather than an e-mail. Generally, a composed, thoughtful letter of appropriate length on paper indicates a seriousness of purpose that you want to present to the CEO of the organization you are writing. Again, your goal in the initial letter is a few paragraphs; your goal in a follow-up letter is perhaps a page-and-a-half. Don't go over two pages under virtually any circumstance; you want the time of very important and very busy people. Taking too long to get to the meat of the issue and to the resolution you would like is a waste of their time; they won't read your letter and you failed.

So, an example of this longer letter. This is a real letter I sent to a collection agency that, as noted earlier, mistakenly sent us a letter it meant to send to someone else [with the same last name apparently] and for whom it did not have a valid address. Perhaps I overreacted but one's credit rating is vital in this modern, information technology, rare person-to-person world. I deleted the name and address; otherwise this is the rest of the letter:

Dear Mr. [DELETED]:

Yesterday, when I came home for lunch, I found a letter from your firm mistakenly addressed to a "John H. Dobbs" at our address. I opened the envelope and found a rather threatening letter about debt collection. I immediately called your company to make clear that there never has been a John H. Dobbs at this address; indeed, I am not related to anyone named John H. Dobbs.

The person to whom I was transferred, NAME DELETED, was not helpful. I am sure that someone at

NAME OF CREDIT AGENCY DELETED took over this "case," checked names and addresses in Ames, and found that there was a Dobbs address. Actually there are several and none of us are related to each other.

I worry about credit ratings and identity theft. I have seen as doubtlessly you have seen the news reports of the trouble people have restoring credit ratings and re-creating identity when something goes wrong. I don't want that to happen to me.

So, let's be clear. Your company sent a letter to the wrong address. It would be different if the last name in question was common, that is, Smith or Jones, Zhang or Garcia. But my last name is not that common. Since my only interaction with your company was this incorrectly addressed letter, I have no reason to feel confident that there isn't a record associating this individual and our address.

I want such assurance that this isn't the case. Please send us a brief letter that your company has disassociated that name and our address and that our address is not in your data bank of deadbeats. I expect a prompt, brief and clear response.

This is clearly not meant as a threat, but I have to protect my credit rating, and if I don't hear from you I will check with the State Attorney General's Office to see if there is recourse; I will write the Sioux City Better Business Bureau to file a complaint, and I will speak with our family attorney how should we pursue the matter.

> *Please, let's close out this situation amicably.*
> *Thank you.*

Charles M. Dobbs

I enclosed a copy of the letter that this particular credit services company sent mistakenly to our address, keeping the original along with a copy of my letter. When the owner responded and provided the written assurance I wanted, I put all of it together in case I should ever need to correct an error on our credit accounts.

Here's an actual copy of a letter we sent our cellular telephone company at that time to complain about incorrect charges after a series of failed efforts with "customer service." Actually, I apparently complained several years ago about something that as of this writing in 2014 has become part of a consent deal with a different cell phone carrier – that is, allowing third party access and charging people for services they did not request and probably did not want. I was just ahead of the curve! Again, I deleted individual names and the company; the rest of the letter follows:

Dear Cellular Telephone Company CEO]

I am writing because, for more than two months, I have been asking your company to correct the errors in our account. To wit:

I have called;

I have texted;

I have e-mailed;

I have written print letters;

I have involved my credit card company, NAME DELETED.

Nothing seems to work.

Permit me to explain. **My wife, Ann, and I signed up for a relatively simple family plan; we each get so many unrestricted minutes per month; we each can send and receive so many text messages; and we each can send and receive so many photographs. The monthly charge, including all taxes, was, for months on end $71.11.** *[bold-face in original letter]*

Then, we received a bill for more than $90.00. Your company claimed we signed up for services – including two services that I simply cannot figure out their respective products and separately something that your company offers that again I cannot understand what it is. We did not want any of these – not Ann, not me. Each time we contacted your company's customer service operation we were assured the *charges would be removed. To be accurate, your customer service operation insisted we contact one of the third party operations to cancel a service that we did not knowingly request, did not want, and that you allowed access to our credit card account, which really doesn't seem fair, does it? Sir, charges are still there. I looked at the account summary on the telephone and it shows a bill due the end of August for more than $80.00.*

Please, what does it take to correct the account? I have tried every reasonable way for more than two months; I have wasted your company's time; I have wasted my time; you can imagine my frustration. Why can't your company provide us only what we requested [when we signed up for our current two year plan at a company store in Valley West Mall in West Des Moines, Iowa] and nothing else? And why can't your company remove these unwanted third party services nearly as fast as it signed us up?

We each have a Samsung Gravity TXT 3G telephone. If you look at one of these phones, they regularly sit "locked." To unlock, one presses the left top button, then hits okay. Sometimes, while locked and not being used [and you can check all the times we don't use our phones], we apparently received unrequested messages from your company and third party providers offering services. In the act of unlocking the phone we may have inadvertently signed up for services. This is wrong. We don't want them.

NAME OF CEO DELETED, please, take a moment, tell an assistant of yours to contact accounts receivable or customer service and fix this. It cannot be that difficult. I am a history professor at Iowa State University but, for 15 years I was the executive assistant and chief of staff for this more than $1 billion organization. If something like this came across my desk, I assure you I knew how to take care of it. If I saw more than one similar complaint, I looked into that part of our operation because the problems might have been more than surface deep.

Finally, sir, please have someone e-mail me a corrected and accurate bill so I can see that your company is only charging us for that which we want which should only total $71.11 a month. Easy-peasy.

Thank you very much.
Charles M. Dobbs

As with the credit services company, I gained the resolution I wanted. Someone in the cellular telephone company's executive offices called to indicate we would receive back credit for overpayments and thereafter the company would charge us correctly and that did happen and we have remained with the company. And had all these companies not allowed such unwanted third party access to cell phone accounts, perhaps they could have avoided the consent decree that the news media recently reported.

Another real world example - my letter about the re-booking of our flights to my niece, Lori's, wedding several years ago. Again, I deleted direct information but the remainder of the letter is as I sent it several years ago.

NAME, TITLE AND ADDRESS DELETED

RE: Travel company Record Locator Number: DELETED
Airline #1 Record Locator Number: DELETED
Airline #2 Record Locator Number: DELETED
Airline #3 Record Locator Number: DELETED
Airline Ticket Numbers: DELETED

Dear Mr. NAME DELETED:

I am writing because you can make right something that is wrong. I purchased plane tickets to fly from Des Moines International Airport [DSM] to Bradley International Airport [BDL] for Saturday, September 24 and to return on Monday, September 26 to attend a family wedding. Your travel services company noted a convenient set of flights, outbound on one major carrier and returning on a different, some smaller carrier. The times were reasonable; the airfare was typical for flying from Des Moines. We thought we were set. Several weeks ago, your company sent an emergency e-mail that I had to call your company directly. The smaller carrier, which business reports have noted is having financial difficulties, announced cutbacks in service, including DSM.

The problem began here with your company. Your customer service representative transferred me and another company representative rep contacted smaller carrier; I was not allowed on the call; he then reported to me that this smaller carrier provided arrangements to fly from BDL just north of I-84 to Dallas-Fort Worth [around I-30] to fly then to Des Moines. I asked at the time why couldn't your company or this smaller carrier put us on flights going directly west, that is, flying out of Hartford-Springfield to Chicago and onto Des Moines, a near straight shot, on either our outbound airline, or another similar, large national carrier. Your agent said that this smaller carrier controlled matters and we had no choice. I assume all this carrier's flight re-routings wore him down. I was disappointed, asked him what I could do, and he indicated I had to contact the third airline to see about a change in flight.

I thought I had no choice. I was wrong; your company did not serve us well.

I went around the circle. I contacted the third carrier where your company gave us a rather roundabout routing, and a customer service rep told me I needed to contact the smaller regional carrier since it made the flight arrangements. I contacted the smaller carrier and I was bounced around but this carrier indicated that since it was the outbound airline's ticket stock, I needed to contact the outbound airline. I called that airline and after getting bounced around several offices its agent indicated I needed to call your company. Back to where I started. Nice, huh?!

The airline's customer service representative transferred me to the internet travel company and the travel company's agent tried the airline again and an airline agent said to contact the airline who was leaving the Des Moines market. That airline apparently agreed, and your rep indicated we could be re-routed on the substitute airline leaving around 10:30 am and arriving in DSM shortly after 3:00 pm. Serendipity. He asked to call me back, apparently spoke more with the airline leaving Des Moines, and called me to indicate that I HAD FORFEITED MY RIGHTS BECAUSE I "AGREED" TO THE FLIGHT THROUGH DALLAS. I TOLD HIM I WAS GIVEN NO CHOICE. HE INDICATED I WAS STUCK AND IT WAS $150.00 PER TICKET TO MAKE A CHANGE.

Mr. DELETED, I believe this is a case of corporate error. Your original agent should have sought to book us either on either of the two national airlines through Chicago or Detroit and not way out of the way through DFW. Through no fault of our own we are forced to waste hours, have a much longer day, and fly through DFW to return home.

You can make this right. While I have returned to my position as professor of history I was, for fifteen years, the assistant to the president at Iowa State University which is a $1 billion, rather complex operation. Among other duties, I served as the final complaint officer before complainants went to the Board of Regents, the state legislature, or the Governor. While I did not always agree with complainants, when complaints made sense, I made them "whole" again. You can do the same. I read your company's "Corporate Code of Conduct" which you publish online. I remember when American business had two rules. Rule No. 1: the customer is always right; Rule No. 2: when in doubt refer to Rule No. 1. I always liked Robert Townsend's <u>Up the Organization</u>; he noted that client dealings with "first responders" made corporate image, not public relations departments.

Mr. DELETED, you can make this right. I did ask when I responded to that initial notification from your company if I had alternatives. Your employee indicated "no." Please change our return booking at your company's expense to the flights we want. You can take lemons, so to speak, and make lemonade. Please have someone book us on UA 637/ UA 807 OR AA 3630/4053 on 9/26.

Thank you very much.
Charles M. Dobbs

Here is yet another one to a casual restaurant chain that has an outlet in Ames, Iowa:

Dear Mr. CEO:

I am writing to express my disappointment with the lack of response from a representative of your restaurant company.

Two Saturdays back my wife and I had lunch at our local restaurant in Ames, Iowa. I ordered the Raspberry Cashew Chicken Salad and she ordered the Strawberry Pecan Chicken Salad; we each asked for the low calorie raspberry vinaigrette.

When our food arrived, I opened the container of salad dressing. It spurted all over my shirt and shorts. Really, I have opened such containers before, and I have been the family cook for more than 40 years, ever since my father died and my mother had to return to work, and picked one of her kids to do the cooking. My wife, seeing what happened to me, opened her container away from her; it also spurted, but not as much as mine.

I give credit to the young woman who brought our food to us. When she saw what happened, she was back in a flash with a wet cloth and new dressing. Good person!

I went on line and sent an e-mail describing what had occurred. I only wanted acknowledgement of what happened to me and perhaps a promise to look into it. I did expect some kind of response. It is now 9 days and nothing, which means I will not be receiving a response.

In 1970, Robert Townsend, then President and CEO of Avis Rent-A-Car Corporation [he was CEO when it came up with the iconic, "we're #2, so we try harder" campaign], authored Up The Organization. It is one of the best books on business I have ever read. He wrote corporate heads should fire their public relations units because first greeters, those people who interact with the public, establish the image of the organization whether intended or not. If you offer the public an opportunity to provide comments, there should be some kind of response, even pro forma.

What if I were wearing a suit, dress shirt and tie? What if it were a woman with a nice dress? What if we had to spend for dry cleaning? What if the dressing left a small but permanent stain? And your staff can't take a moment to respond? Shame.

I am disappointed and I wanted you to know. Thank you.

Respectfully,

Charles M. Dobbs

Not surprisingly, a representative from that restaurant company called within a few days.

Here is a similarly redacted letter I sent the parent media company of the local newspaper whose change in subscription options and rates disappointed me and whose publisher did not respond to an earlier inquiry/complaint.

Dear Large Media Company CEO:

Several weeks ago the president and publisher of our regional newspaper sent a letter to subscribers with what she called good news. She indicated that too many people had dropped their respective subscriptions to the print edition of the newspaper and were reading the paper, or what they wanted to read in the paper, on line and for free. Obviously, this had a serious and negative impact on the company's bottom line.

All well and good.

She then indicated that, for existing subscribers to the print edition, whether we wanted or not, we had to pay some 23% more once our existing subscriptions ran out, to maintain our print subscription and to have the capacity to read the newspaper on internet capable telephones, on I-Pads and other tablet devices, and on notebook computers. My wife and I have none of those; we do not desire the capacity to read the newspaper in any format save for a printed newspaper.

It seems your central Iowa newspaper and by extension your media company decided to penalize existing print subscribers rather than find a means to make those "lurkers" reading on line pay for the content they should not receive free.

I wrote this to our newspaper's publisher. I indicated my disappointment; I further indicated that we did not want the current, truncated newspaper at an increased price and with electronic access we will not use. I concluded that we would not renew our subscription. She chose not to respond. I assumed the lack of response indicated that she had received too many letters and telephone calls of complaint.

This policy could not have originated with our local newspaper. Either your office originated it or approved it as a test.

I am writing to ask that, when you conclude it has failed, please come up with a menu plan. For those of us who want only the printed newspaper, let us continue to pay only *for that option; for those who want all those electronic doo-hickies, charge them more.*

*I believe this policy was shortsighted, would have failed any honest review with a cross-section of existing subscribers **and** counting both the increased revenue from those who pay even though they won't access the electronic versions and the decreased revenue from people like us your company will receive less income from its newspapers across the state of Iowa.*

Thank you.
Respectfully,

Charles M. Dobbs

Unsurprisingly, the publisher of our regional newspaper then found the time to call me. The national company was unwilling to adjust its subscription pricing tiers, and many central Iowans cancelled their subscriptions to the newspaper as did residents of other cities for their local newspapers which this large national media company owned. It's a shame, really. A morning newspaper is a wonderful addition to one's breakfast but why force a dwindling subscription base to purchase electronic access that many newspaper readers neither want nor need?

CHAPTER EIGHT

In general, be polite

I realize this shows me to be the old man that I am. But in recent years I bristle inside when students e-mail me either with the greeting "hey," or "dude," or use my first name or don't use any name or title at all. I am three times their age; I have reached an educational level they haven't, is it so difficult for them to address me as Professor or Dr. Dobbs? And don't they think I might be more agreeable if they show some common courtesy and respect for rank and achievement? I know it is a generational thing, but show respect.

When my sister Debbie and I were little, our parents taught us to stand up when our elders and our betters entered the room. If you want to shock someone, do that. Their eyes will open widely, and perhaps a thin smile on the lips, and that person will think you are the nicest individual he or she has met in weeks.

Courtesy is the language of strangers and, when you approach a company or organization for resolution, you are a stranger. Be polite. Historically, it means you are not a threat and so the person you are addressing can relax and not fear for his or her person. There is a much disputed story that Napoleon changed continental Europe from passing on the left, keeping one's right hand free to greet or to fight, to passing on the right to spur commerce and comity. It is disputed, but there is a point to being polite if only to follow the Golden Rule that virtually every religion has a version.

Years ago we had purchased plane tickets to fly to south Florida to visit my mother over Labor Day weekend. As luck would have it, a bad hurricane hit the area – it's south Florida, after all, and early September is near the height of hurricane season – and the airlines cancelled all flights into Miami, Fort Lauderdale, and West Palm Beach airports. Obviously I was disappointed, but I called airline to ask what would happen next. A very nice woman represented the company and we talked. It certainly wasn't her fault that the hurricane hit when we intended to travel; the airline could not make the air safe for its planes; sometimes this kind of thing happens. After a while, this airline customer agent thanked me for being pleasant about it all and I told her it wasn't her fault [or her company's]. Why get angry? She arranged for us to fly another weekend at the same airfare, which otherwise was not available for the weekend I chose. It was very nice of her, and I thanked her profusely.

She responded that she was an older employee [we were about the same age] and a couple of days earlier her employer had declared bankruptcy and cut pensions about 90%. This person had been counting on that pension, a promise for many years on the job, and suddenly she had to contemplate working years longer either for her company or another employer. That was a tough blow and then to have to deal with people angry with her because the hurricane cancelled their flights?

So, when you are thinking of venting your anger either in person [think back to the passenger who, after landing in Des Moines, yelled unfairly and inappropriately at the local baggage claim clerk], on the telephone [this airline customer agent] or in a letter, remember that most of the people you encounter are absolutely innocent in your situation and have their own lives, own situations, and own problems with which to deal. There's no reason to add to their stress, and it won't help you gain the resolution you seek anyways.

BE POLITE.

In writing, use the phrase "thank you" once although don't beat it to death. Use polite grammatical constructions – e.g., "I hope you will review the situation I have described and take an action," Don't insist, don't threaten, and don't be rude. If that is the route you want to follow, engage an attorney and seek a confrontational resolution which means you don't need this book.

Back to students, you don't want to complain the way some students ask for a favor. My favorite e-mail was a student who wrote to indicate he had an opening in his schedule, my class was "convenient" for him to take, and he wanted me to open a closed class – which meant it was very popular with students who quickly claimed all the available seats – for him. He didn't ask me to open a seat; he didn't indicate an interest in the subject matter which, since it was History, was very interesting, indeed; he didn't recognize he was asking a favor. He figured he had it coming; to him, my only reasonable response was to admit him. Well, I didn't open the class to provide a seat for him.

There is something about showing common courtesy. Don't be the lout in Des Moines baggage claim; be nice. In this case, the student in question could have written indicating he wanted to take the class; the class "closed" before he could sign up; he was interested in the subject matter or he could write that he had heard I was a good classroom instructor [I am] and schmoozed a little to ask his favor. What did Julie Andrews sing in *Mary Poppins* (1964) – "just a spoonful of sugar helps the medicine go down."

On the other hand, in a subsequent semester a student e-mailed me nicely, explained why she hadn't signed up earlier, why she was interested in the course, she had tried to add it in earlier semesters and it always closed quickly and she was near graduation. I signed her "add" form. Best of all, she had the high grade in the class on the first quiz even though she missed a week of lecture – a terrific outcome for all concerned.

Write with a smile. ☺

This is not exactly on task, but, it is necessary if you want to achieve a positive outcome from your complaint.

Our daughter, Hannah, was dating a nice young man, Matthew, and after they had dated for a while, his mother wanted to meet her. The two of them drove to the Quad Cities from Ames to meet his mom, and after a meal and some time together, Hannah told her boyfriend's mother and now her mother-in-law that she was so happy to meet her because now she realized why Matthew was so nice and why she liked him so much [because of his mother and the way she raised him ☺]. Pretty smart, yes?! Well, write like that!

Finally, if you gain the resolution you want or you are willing to accept, write a thank you note. Don't let the conversation end with the CEO or someone that he or she asks to respond writing to offer some compensation and regrets. Let that respondent know you appreciate his or her time and the offer. While this won't affect the response you received, it may well help the next person who writes that company or organization if the person handling the situation feels the complainant appreciates his or her time and effort.

It's a kind of *karma*.

You are not writing to help your situation; you are writing to help the next person to write that individual or that office. You want the person who interceded or acted on your behalf to realize that you did appreciate the action he or she took [because you ought to appreciate people doing the right thing]. If you write, then it is easier for the next person to complain since the recipient of your complaint will understand that his/her intercession was much appreciated, and so on until the circle comes back to you.

And this note should be brief, no more than a paragraph, just an acknowledgement of their action and your appreciation.

I always appreciated the people who complained to the President's Office[s] and who, after I offered a resolution that pleased them, wrote to express their appreciation. At my previous institution, there was a young woman who signed up for classes, then realized she didn't have financing, and dropped everything. The institution charged her for registering, for dropping later than a deadline it established, and indicated it would turn the account over to collections. She didn't realize there were various deadlines for dropping courses and the longer one took to drop courses or dis-enroll, the more money the University wanted.

Father and daughter came to speak with me, and it was clear that she would have been a first-generation college student had she registered and made some mistakes in timing but really wasn't at fault. They had no prior experience with college and with college financing and billing. I voided the debt because it seemed an honest mistake, we had provided no real service [and thus had incurred no real expenses], and I didn't see family capacity to pay this bill. [She would have had to borrow to finance virtually all of her college expenses.] Several weeks later the father came to visit me; he brought a paperweight he had made in his garage thanking me. I still use in my office in my current institution. I really appreciated that he appreciated what we did for his family.

Some years ago an engineering student at Iowa State decided to audit my American military history course. He was a terrific student and would have earned an "A" had he taken the course for credit. One evening, his mother called me; she was a local school teacher; his father was a faculty member in another department of the University. It was one of the nicest telephone calls I have ever received. She said she realized teachers rarely receive compliments and she wanted me to know when her son would come home for Sunday dinner with his parents about the thing about school he discussed was my class. I thanked her profusely. I was walking on air for days. Say "thanks" when it is merited; you like to receive praise and appreciation, and so do others.

CHAPTER NINE

How to find contact information for the CEO

The Internet has transformed the flow of information. Several decades ago, if one wanted information on a company, the name of the CEO, and/ or a good mailing address, one would have typically gone to one's local public library, spoke with a reference librarian, and looked up information on the company or organization. It might have taken several efforts to find the right address, the name of the CEO or investor relations office, etc. Of course, the source might be old, the information outdated. But between Value Line™ and other corporate directories, one could usually find the name of the current or at least a recent CEO and an accurate mailing address.

Times have changed! While public libraries are great places to frequent and reference librarians are outstanding and deserve our appreciation [please note, I am married to a terrific reference librarian! ☺], one can find a great deal of information through the Internet. However, there are times when it is worth your time to visit your public library and to speak with one of the reference professionals. And be sure to thank them for their assistance; they'll really appreciate it!

Let's begin with a general search. At your favorite search engine, type in the name of the company. Check the suggested web site for "Contact Us." That frequently leads you to the public relations unit; sometimes that's a good thing; sometimes it is a layer between you and a real response to the question you raised.

I like to check the hot link "For Investors" or "Investor Relations." Usually these last two will yield corporate information, including the names and proper titles of corporate officers – the Holy Grail for your complaint letter. You should find the major corporate officers, e.g., CEO, COO, President, and the Board of Directors or the Board's Executive Committee along with contact information for the corporate office. You don't like folks who misspell [or mispronounce] your name. Be sure to copy name and title accurately. Use that title when addressing the letter, e.g., Dear President So-and-So.

Sometimes it can be difficult to find the information you want. Play with your computer and you'll find it. Search the web for news stories; try different versions of the corporate name. It could be the firm has a legal name and does business under another name. It could be the firm is a holding company of a sort for various divisions, much as Darden Restaurants, Inc. is a holding company for a family of well-known restaurants that once included Red Lobster, Olive Garden, Capital Grille and Longhorn Steakhouse among others. Companies certainly don't want to waste the valuable time of their respective CEOs with frivolous complaints, so they don't always put such contact information front and center.

If you become frustrated, as noted before visit your local public library and acquaint yourself with the reference or information services librarian. He or she is trained, experienced, and happy to help you. Actually, in the interest of fair disclosure, it's not just that my wife, Ann, is an outstanding reference librarian, her father was until he retired and her brother is. It's a family business! But reference librarians are an important resource in your search for the right person, the one who can say "yes," to resolve your situation.

Standard finding aids include *Standard & Poor's Register of Corporations* and *Dun & Bradstreet Directory.* There is also the Consumer Action Web Site of the Federal Citizen Information Center which is free and provides corporate addresses, toll-free phone numbers and Web sites to companies but some of the contact information leads you to customer relations sites, not CEO offices. You may also try *Yahoo's Finance's* pages or a similar web site which captures news reports of various companies and oftentimes quotes or cites the corporate or organizational CEO.

If searching through a corporate web site does not yield the appropriate information, just type in the name of the company and the phrase "CEO" or "president" at your search prompt. Usually the responses will include news stories that contain the name of the CEO; then go to an online telephone directory, e.g., www.switchboard.com, and in looking for the telephone number you'll find the corporate mailing address. CEOs typically want to be good corporate citizens; they volunteer their time for important community projects; they serve on local, regional, and state associations; they hold their positions in part because they accept the need to be in the public eye. You can find them . . . use those research skills you learned in school.

Finally, on one occasion, I wrote the "Investor Relations" link to ask for the CEOs name, proper title, and mailing address and provided a very brief indication of why I wanted the address. Someone rather promptly provided it. Some customer service sites as well as some investor relations sites will give you contact information for the corporate CEO.

If you would rather e-mail than send a print letter, this trick of a sort may help you. If you can figure out any one employee's e-mail address, e.g., <u>cdobbs@iastate.edu</u>, then you can see the pattern for others. You might write the president of Iowa State University at first letter of first name last name @iastate.edu. You may have to play around with full first names, first name initial, etc. but it likely will yield a proper address. Sometimes one can simply e-mail president@ or CEO@ and the company's e-mail extension although this likely will default to an assistant but hopefully in the CEO's central office.

So, no excuses and no worries – you can do it between your own resources, your local public library's resources, and asking for help from the company or organization you want to contact.

AND REMEMBER TO . . .

Be sure you remember to provide appropriate contact information. If you are complaining through a company web site, be sure to supply your name and either a mailing address, telephone number, or e-mail address. Certainly, if you are writing a letter [which I generally prefer to do], be sure to provide your return address atop the letter as we were all taught in typing class many, many decades ago. Sign your name as you wish to be addressed. If you want someone to call, don't just provide a telephone number, indicate times when you will be available. You might want to give your cell phone number rather than a home telephone so the company can reach you more easily. And, if you give out a telephone number, answer it. Recognize that corporate or organizational phone number in case you are just chatting with a friend or using your smartphone as a games machine.

Make yourself easily available for a telephone response or risk failing in your objective. Put differently, if you make yourself hard to reach, you likely will wind up frustrated. How many times do you think busy people will try to reach you before they give up and move on to another task?

CHAPTER TEN

You do not/can not do

Don't threaten.

Let me repeat that . . . ***don't threaten***.

It's not just the sad reality of our post-9/11 environment, too many school shootings, a ridiculous reluctance to enforce real gun control, and a seeming disregard for our common humanity. Threatening is counter-productive.

Don't ever threaten or intimate physical harm. There is no need for further discussion. Don't do it. You deserve whatever subsequently happens should you so threaten. I hope the police explain the situation clearly to you as they take you away.

This is silly, but at my previous institution a student came to see me one day and said, "I want to shoot you." For the next several weeks I had a baseball bat – my old Louisville Slugger™ - under my desk. I figured - or hoped! - I could hit him over the head before he could pull the gun out of his bag. When he returned he made it clear he meant to take my picture and I relaxed my grip. But until that point I didn't want to take chances.

Next, let's deal with the milder, more reasonable situation first. You are disappointed with a service you received or a product you purchased. You find the proper mailing address for the corporate CEO and you send a well-composed letter. Don't escalate the situation. Don't write something like, "if you don't give me satisfaction I will never frequent your establishment again." In terms of the "cost" of dealing with you as a customer or client, the business might just decide it can prosper without you. Yes, if after complaining and not receiving satisfaction you might conclude as I have concluded in only a couple of situations that I would not do business again with that company. But I didn't lead off threatening to never do business with them again.

Some years ago, the parents of a non-resident Iowa State student wrote the President's Office to complain. I looked into the situation and learned that the academic advisor had properly advised the student and she decided quite on her own to take a science course sequence somewhat beyond her background and abilities. She was a "major," not a "minor" in age [over age 18] and had the right to disregard the advisor's suggestion about a somewhat easier sequence to fulfill the general education requirement for the sciences. And while she did not do well in that more difficult course sequence, it was her choice.

I wrote the parents that I could not discuss their child's situation without her express approval [again student privacy legislation] but I hinted my sense that the University had acted correctly. They called on separate telephones and began complaining to me and arguing with each other at the same time. I put my telephone down for a while and did some work as they argued. They even argued with each other whether I had put the telephone receiver down!

I guessed the real issue for them was the cost of tuition for a non-resident student – their daughter – and perhaps they were having some difficult financial times – this was right after the dot.com bust in the stock market – and wanted to bring their daughter home for resident tuition at a good home-state university. I sent a brief note to the Associate Vice President for Enrollment Services, a really good person who transformed the University's student recruitment operation, that I didn't think it was worth the cost of trying to retain the student given the parents. He hated to give up on any tuition-payer – after all, he was an Admissions professional – but agreed they were difficult and perhaps it was best to let her go.

And let's conclude with the tougher though still reasonable situation. You write your letter and you note that, fundamentally if the organization or company does not agree with you and respond promptly, your lawyer will be in touch.

Boy, I loved when people wrote the president or said over the telephone at either of my two institutions that they would follow-up with legal action. Both universities had first-rate legal counsel and when someone threatened legal action, I passed the matter to these excellent advocates. The opportunity for a low-keyed, non-confrontational resolution had passed and equally important most likely the person writing did not do better dealing with our legal counsel than had s/he dealt with me. Silly.

Actually, when someone threatened to turn the matter over to attorneys whether real or imagined, I would tell them that I had to bow out, and that usually caused them to back off from contacting the attorney. It's easier to resolve situations in a collegial manner rather than an adversarial one, and lawyers necessarily exist in an adversarial situation. So it goes.

I do admit that in some cases I asked the university attorneys to review the response I wanted to send to be sure I didn't give unnecessary offense or possibly make their job more difficult if the recipient of my letter subsequently chose to sue.

CHAPTER ELEVEN

Write a letter of appreciation
[for good service or a good deed]

If you decide to write letters to complain when you are disappointed, you need to balance that with an equal propensity to write when you are pleased by something out of the ordinary. It is *karma, yin-yang,* or Newtonian physics – either it helps to go around the circle OR it is the balance to tilting too far one way or the other. Frankly, if you write to appreciate something good, it gives you "permission" to write to complain about something that was unsatisfactory.

Several years ago my younger niece married. It was a nice outdoor ceremony at a bucolic scene by a lake and a nice dinner at a nearby hotel/restaurant near Amherst, Massachusetts. My sister approved a dairy-heavy menu and I don't digest dairy. I asked the waitress serving our table not to bring me much of the meal because I dislike wasting food and I couldn't eat most of the previously-selected menu.

Well, the waitress was terrific. She obviously told the person handling the wedding dinner and/or the head chef about my situation and I received a separate meal which I greatly appreciated. I thanked her and privately tipped her above and beyond what must have been included in the bill my sister paid for all of the wait staff. I also wrote the owner and the head chef to thank them since such flexibility is really and truly above and beyond the call of duty. [And the owner responded that the restaurant was always willing to make such accommodation - a terrific attitude!] I am sure it is a very successful business with such a positive attitude towards its guests.

In another instance, several years ago I forgot my mother's boyfriend's birthday. It was my fault; he is a wonderful person and has made my mom happy for many, many years [as she has made him happy]. I was an idiot. And my mom pointed that out very clear to me over the telephone during our regular Sunday morning phone call.

I sat down with my laptop to check on bakeries and groceries near my mother. It was a Sunday and many of the specialty bakeries were closed; I called one rather upscale grocery store and the bakery manager indicated they did not deliver [I lived about a thousand miles from my mom; I was stuck. I called a store of a regional grocery chain in south Florida. The bakery manager was a G-dsend. I explained the situation; I asked if perhaps I could purchase a cake from the chill case, have her add "Happy Birthday, Marty," and have someone drive it to my mother's apartment, several miles away and charge me for everything.

What a manager! She not only added "happy birthday" to a cake and dispatched two young employees to deliver the cake; she gave them a couple of happy birthday balloons and they loudly sang happy birthday to Marty on the catwalk of the condominium complex. All their neighbors learned it was his birthday and he received many happy birthday greetings. My mom thought I had planned this all along and had deliberately strung her along on the telephone earlier that morning. From lemons to lemonade owing to one terrific person!

I wrote this largely southern U.S. grocery chain corporate office that evening to thank the bakery manager in the store not too far from my mother's apartment and the next time we visited my mom, I went to that store to thank the bakery manager in person. It was worth the bill for the cake, balloons, and the time of the two employees for what she did to make up for my forgetfulness.

Some thirty years ago, a work colleague and I flew to Santa Ana/John Wayne airport for a conference at a nearby hotel. I normally sleep well even on the road but for some reason I didn't on this trip. I walked downstairs around 2:30 in the morning just to sit. The night desk clerk was a wonderful person and perhaps appreciated someone with whom to speak. Regardless, over the next few hours he offered me freshly-made coffee and later, when he went back to the kitchens to get a fresh pastry for himself, he brought me one; he let me read all the newspapers they had for sale once the gift shop opened.

I thanked him for each kindness and he said each time, "well, it's a Hilton." I thanked the morning manager later, and he said, "It's a Hilton." I wrote Hilton to thank the CEO and got a reply thanking me for my letter but noting, "It's a Hilton." You can guess where I stay when we travel and when I have any kind of positive experience with any organization I often think to myself "well, it's a Hilton." By the way, soon thereafter, the hotel owners changed its franchise affiliation but my loyalty to Hilton hotels remains.

And, frankly, wouldn't you like to receive a letter for something you did well? Several years ago as one of my course assignments, I was teaching the department's senior research seminar course which is required of all graduating seniors in History. A few days after students had submitted the final drafts of their term research papers, one student stopped in to see me. She said she had some very fine teachers and some not-so-fine teachers at Iowa State and she wanted to give thank-you notes to the four or five best, and she then handed me one. It made my day. It made up for all the stupidities of students unwilling be accept accountability for their actions. Cloud nine!

And, more recently, my wife, Ann, son, Jonathan, and I were at our local Sam's club looking for something our daughter, Hannah, could not find at her local club in Dallas. We thought we saw it on a pallet well overhead. I asked a young employee if he could help us. Within a few minutes, he was coming over with a small lift and another employee came to help him. We got the merchandise, our daughter was happy, and I wrote to Sam's Club to thank the manager who obviously trained staff well and these two young men for being so nice. I learned from an e-mail from the store manager that there is an internal rewards process at Sam's Club as probably many other employers have and he would see to it that these two earned points - all in all, a nice outcome.

Years ago, Continental Airlines had what it called an "orchids and onions" process; cabin attendants had forms which had the title, "Orchids and Onions." Continental consciously provided a way for passengers to provide feedback on its ground and airborne operations. More than once I filled out a form to thank a cabin attendant for something above and beyond the ordinary. Continental used these submitted forms to provide small rewards to such outstanding employees.

Many good companies have similar internal reward systems.

Several years ago we stayed at Homewood Suites across the street from Mall of America. When we checked in, the front desk person was friendly, competent, and informative. After our visit, I received an e-mail from Hilton's HHonors© operation asking about our stay. As part of my response to the questionnaire, I wrote about this excellent employee. A day later I received an e-mail from the hotel manager that he wanted me to know he would reward her as part of that company's so-called orchids and onions operation.

Something similar happened in a way with my complaint about the cake from Hy-Vee given the terrific and wonderful response from the store manager who subsequently received the "store director of the year" award from the Hy-Vee company. It happened with the two young employees at our local Sam's Club who were so nice to us the day before Christmas. And again it happened with the restaurant where my niece had her wedding dinner.

It's good to say "thank you" when warranted. People deserve praise when they do well; after all, you like to receive praise and as I noted earlier I think offering such praise gives one the "right" to complain when treatment, product, or situations are not up to the quality one has a right to expect.

CHAPTER TWELVE

Complaining in person

Complaining in person is very different from complaining in writing. In the isolation of writing a letter, one can compose oneself, keep one's emotions controlled, check one's argument and facts, edit one's writing, and in general have time to make an effective case.

Complaining face-to-face places a premium on live time interpersonal skills. One has to organize the argument, arrange the facts, maintain one's composure, and interact with an individual all in real time. There are issues of the image one presents, how one speaks, how one stands.

Part of the issue of complaining in person reflects personality type. A brief discussion of personality type may be useful. There are many so-called personality indicators, but my favorite is the Myers-Briggs Type Indicator®. Building on the work of famed psychologist Carl Jung, Katherine Cook Briggs and her daughter, Isabel Briggs Myers, studied people and proposed four scales to help better understand personality differences. Each of the scales represents values along a continuum and reflects how people draw energy – what takes less energy and therefore is more comfortable to do and what takes more energy and thus what one is less likely to do. Some people have strong preferences – they are comfortable in some situations and less comfortable in others; some people do not have as defined a set of preferences and are more comfortable in more kinds of situations - both professional and personal.

Briggs and Myers developed one scale focusing on extraversion and intraversion [they did spell both words with an "a" and not an "o" for they refined the definition of both words]. Some people, perhaps 70% or more of the population, draw energy interacting with people; they are likely to speak first and speak a lot. They may dominate conversations; they may not listen well. A smaller percentage, perhaps 30% or less, are intraverts;

they are reflective thinkers, they are more likely to be quiet in big groups, more likely to observe rather than interact. They may think the next day about what they could/should have said the day before.

Those favoring extraversion [and it is a continuum where some extraverts are outgoing in more situations and others are that way in fewer] would find speaking up easier. However, they may not listen as well, notice cues from the store manager, and thus achieve a satisfactory resolution. Pausing to listen helps extraverts.

Those favoring intraversion may not react well to a dynamic situation – intraverts regularly think to themselves "well, if that situation recurs, here's what I should have said." Intraverts will do better if they make brief notes and organize their thoughts – at least their main points – before they begin speaking with the store manager. Having a script if only a mental check list helps intraverts.

Another MBTI continuum contrasts "judging" and "perceiving." Some people, about half of the population, are "judgers." They come to closure easily; strong "Js" may want to bring the matter – whatever it is – to a quick conclusion after the first good point rather than listening to all the alternatives. Or, these strong "judgers" may have decided not only that their complaint is just but so is their proposed resolution, and they won't listen to alternatives from a store manager or other personnel.

Some people, again about half of the population, are "perceivers." They see possibilities, and have more problems coming to closure. Imagine a couple where one is a strong "J" and the other a strong "P" and they need to decide where to eat out that evening. The J will decide quickly – "let's get pizza at Giovanni's" – and want to move on; the P will want to weigh all the possibilities – "we had pizza last week; what else is there?" Each can, to an extent, frustrate the other. In our case, a J may accept the first proposal the manager or person in charge proposes or may be stuck on the resolution he or she is seeking. A perceiver may be more open to discussion, to feeling around the situation, to working out a compromise, or, perhaps, may want to hold out hoping for something better.

One of the presidents for whom I worked was as strong a "judger" as he was an "introvert." If a member of the President's Cabinet raised an issue for discussion and, especially for advice, this president accepted the first good idea proposed and shut off further conversation. He liked closure as a "J" and he liked to end meetings quickly as an "I." The real result was that many Cabinet members stopped bringing ideas to this group of senior leaders for discussion preferring to discuss them in smaller group settings and then come to the president with a formal proposal.

I heard from a colleague who served a president at a different research university that she would not stay with a decision she reached. In one instance, he noted that she changed her mind before he literally reached the door to leave her office. It was a commonplace event. Within a year or so of reporting to her, he moved on to another university finding it more comfortable to report to someone who was more decisive, more of a "J" and less of a "P."

Ann likes to watch the HGTV program, "House Hunters." One evening the show featured a couple where the wife had looked at more than 200 homes - pity that real estate agent! - searching for the absolutely perfect home. She worried, if she decided on one house, she might miss a more perfect one. Meanwhile, they didn't have a home for themselves or their children. At some point, unless one has unlimited funds and time, the perfect home doesn't exist. Life is a compromise; make a decision. That's easy for me to say because I am a reasonably strong "J" and the wife on this particular episode was clearly an overwhelmingly strong "P" always hoping for a better alternative.

Without beating this to death in such a brief discussion, and ever more inaccurate presentation of an interesting theory about psychological type in a longer discussion, regardless of the absolute worth of the MBTI and other, similar instruments, people have different comfort levels and different abilities when interacting face-to-face. You probably know your strengths and weaknesses already but you absolutely need to know your comfort level before you choose to interact. What if you become easily frustrated when the situation, whatever the situation is, doesn't go your way; you may lose your self-control and speak or act in a manner that frankly isn't appropriate or acceptable? What if you can't react in real time when the manager responds to your complaint or issue? If any of this seems stressful, then face-to-face communication may not be your strong suit.

With this preface aside, let's discuss some real face-to-face complaints and how they turned out.

Here's one that went extremely well. Some years ago, I returned from an on-campus meeting and, as I walked into the suite for the President's office, there were some 30 students standing around the executive secretary's desk; they were polite but they were insistent; and she seemed nervous. I walked up, introduced myself, asked if I could help them, and I moved the group into our conference room and invited them to sit down. They were Computer Science majors and wanted to speak with the president about hiring more faculty members for their department. They claimed that, as first year students, Computer Science classes filled before they could enroll; they claimed the same as sophomores; they claimed the same as juniors, and now as seniors they were annoyed. They first complained to the department academic advisors who told them that the president assigned all faculty positions, so they should go to the president's office.

The advisors were absolutely wrong; the University had largely college-based budgeting, but the students deserved a hearing. I listened and promised them I would look into the matter and get back to them in a few days. They complained politely; they presented a clear and seemingly compelling case – more students wanting classes yet the same number of faculty and classes.

I checked into the situation looking back at the department over the past ten years – budget books, course schedules, student enrollments. The students were right. Enrollments had increased steadily every year; the number of faculty remained constant so the number of courses and available seats remained constant. Interestingly, the

College of Liberal Arts and Sciences had overall flat enrollments during that period. Some departments taught more students and some taught fewer yet there were no changes in the number of assigned faculty members per department. That is, several successive arts and sciences college deans apparently failed to take vacant positions from a department or departments whose enrollments were declining to move them to departments where enrollments were increasing.

I wrote this all up for the president, suggested he have the provost speak with the dean about the value of and need for reassigning faculty lines in some situations, and put it in his in-box and moved on to something else. Ten minutes later the president walked into my office [next door to his] and seemed upset. Although colleges had their own budgets and that dean should have reassigned vacant positions from departments whose student enrollments had fallen to departments whose student enrollments were increasing, he was so concerned about the increasing enrollments in Computer Science that he had provided funds from a small reserve he controlled for several new positions. He wanted to know what happened to the funds he had transferred.

I looked further into the matter and found there were two issues. Again, several CLAS deans did not move positions from one department to another to reflect changing student interests and the Provost's Office sat on the president's fund transfer rather than authorizing the department to make the hires. It wanted to use the funds to cover shortfalls if indeed the academic division faced shortfalls rather than meet the needs of students in this high-demand department.

We got the matter resolved, new faculty joined the department, and the students were pleased. I always thought this a model way to complain. And, a new dean in that college changed the policy so that all faculty lines, when vacant, reverted to the college administration so that the dean could help move positions around to reflect student demand and research opportunities. A department with a faculty member who retired or moved on to a job elsewhere had to make the case for the dean to return the position. Higher education is a business even if the model is somewhat different from for-profit business and it needs to employ good business practices such as feed the growing fields.

In my own case, some years ago we all went to a diner for dinner after a day of shopping in Des Moines. I always liked the turkey "blue plate special" featured at the diner. After a while, the waiter brought three meals, and then came back with my daughter's BLT. The toast was badly burned; Hannah looked at me; I asked the waiter about the burnt toast. The manager came over and offered to "comp" the meal. I disagreed. I didn't want her to eat the burnt BLT free; I wanted to pay for a good BLT. I suggested he, the manager, tell the expeditor in the kitchen to move redoing Hannah's meal to the front of the line so she would be eating as we were eating and not after we finished. Again, a complaint doesn't mean getting something free; it means getting what you originally wanted and also suggesting the operation – in this case, a restaurant – check its product before giving it out to customers. The expeditor could/should have noted the burnt, blackened toast and quickly grabbed two new pieces, reconstructed the sandwich and brought it to us.

And, as I wrote in the introduction, there was the case of my son, Jonathan, and the national clothing store in Coralville, Iowa. He asked – politely but insistently – why the clerk treated him differently than two customers ahead of him, and the manager recognized he needed to act quickly to resolve the situation.

Very recently my daughter had a flat tire on her vehicle and she went to the local outlet of a national tire company in Dallas, Texas for a replacement. Several days later she checked prices on line and ordered three more tires from the company. The company's web site promised that her local store would have those tires and at the price noted on the web site in several days. December became January and no tires. Finally Hannah received notice that the store received the tires from the warehouse. When her husband took the vehicle to the store, the store did not have the tires and tried to sell tires that combined cost several hundred more dollars. Hannah complained and the store matched the price of the tires she had wanted.

That was nice. The next day she drove the vehicle to work and realized something was amiss. One tire was flat. She filled up the tire, drove to the store, and pointed out the problem. The manager, a good person, told her that he had used the example of her online tire order to retrain the entire staff how to deal with such orders - part of which was to ensure the store had ordered the proper tires from the regional warehouse. He checked the tire in question and found staff had incorrectly mounted it. He had staff take off all four tires, rebalance them, and remount them. He is a good person; Hannah thanked him - a serendipitous outcome for the store and my daughter.

Contrast these in-person complaints – civil, orderly, and informed – with another one that did little for the complainant. It was a wintry day – which in Iowa means snow, strong winds, and cold weather. A young woman came to the President's Office to complain. Apparently she parked her car on a city street, Beach Avenue, near campus which, in going to school at Iowa State, she had to know that there was no parking on either side of that street and that the street had a towing ordinance during snowy times. The snow storm came; her car blocked efficient snow removal, and the city contacted a towing company to remove it. She had a ticket, the tow charge, and a storage charge at the towing company's yard. She was mad, and she was yelling.

I came out of my office to speak with her. She blamed the university for her predicament; she demanded the university offer to tow student cars parked on city streets so she could avoid a ticket in the future. I had to tell her that Iowa has a very strict, "non-competing" law which meant that the public universities, for example, could not offer a service off campus that private interests could offer. So the ISU Police Department's "help van" was restricted to assisting people on campus. I suggested she could have parked in nearby stadium lots for free and taken the free circulator bus to campus rather than leaving her car on Beach Avenue. She didn't care; she yelled at me and insisted that we, the President's Office, go to the state legislature to lobby for a change in the law. State institutions carry out laws the legislature passes and the governor signs; we don't make law. She left as angry as she came – a very ineffective complaint.

Sometimes the complainant is unreasonable and the institutional representative is a saint. Several years ago we had dinner at the local outlet of a national, casual restaurant chain in Ames. A family at a table next to us called for the manager. The husband complained that his dinner didn't have enough chicken; the manager arranged for a substitute meal with more chicken; the husband complained the meal didn't have enough Alfredo sauce; the manager arranged for more. The couple complained about everything; the manager was as accommodating as one could be, in fact, more so.

I assumed the couple was trying to get a meal for free by complaining. Since our receipt asked us to go online to fill out a customer survey, I wrote about the wonderful shift manager, all that he faced in dealing with this difficult family, and that he deserved some kind of bonus or raise to reflect his calm, accommodating demeanor. Don't complain in person simply to get something for free. Sometimes you just don't like the meal; that happens; move along. And don't complain simply to see if you can force an accommodating manager to gift you what you don't deserve. That ultimately makes it more difficult for those with a good case to gain the resolution they deserve.

You also need to be clear in communicating in person. At my previous institution, one day a student came to the President's Office and after a while said he wanted "to shoot me" when he returned. I am not a particularly brave or adventurous individual; the next day I brought an aluminum baseball bat to keep under my desk. I figured if someone wanted to do me harm, perhaps I could hit him over the head with the bat before anything happened. The student returned a few days later, seemed calmer, and took a camera out of his backpack. As Strother Martin famously said [though often misquoted] in *Cool Hand Luke* [1967], "what we have here is failure to communicate." [Martin never included "a" in the phrase although many since have incorrectly said "a failure."] Each of us probably would have enjoyed the exchange more if he had communicated more clearly.

Sometimes you are not angry and you are organized in your thoughts but the way you stand, the way you speak, the image you present seems to suggest you are angry. You give off an impression you did not intend. Here's something I did that has been the subject of discussion with my daughter over the years. Hannah was still in high school when one Sunday morning, about

7:00 am, I went to a bagel outlet in Ames that was part of a national chain. I wanted to buy a half dozen onion bagels to take home. One of the young people working that morning told me they didn't have any onion bagels. I asked if they had sold out that early and he commented they didn't receive any white dough from the central store bakery in Des Moines, about 45 miles away – so no plain bagels, no onion bagels, and no garlic bagels. I spoke perhaps too quickly, and asked if someone had thought to call the central store in Des Moines to come to Ames with that white dough from which they could make half of the bagels they normally had for sale on such a busy morning. No response. I left dissatisfied.

The next evening my daughter came at me. She said that the two boys were high school classmates of hers; she said they made fun of her for how out of control I was – sadly, we look too much alike which isn't what most daughters want; she claimed she probably couldn't return to school . . . ever! I responded that I never raised my voice; I didn't yell; I was just disappointed that the morning shift workers displayed no initiative in not calling the main store to tell the regional manager they were so lacking in a key product.

Some years later, my daughter, by then a student at Iowa State, came into the President's Office, slammed my office door shut [shocking the clerical staff], looked at me, and said rather loudly, "dad, the same people who piss you off piss me off!" I told her that, yes, she had my personality which really meant my father's personality, and I was sorry about that. She then noted that sometimes people thought she was upset when she was just taking in a situation. It's the way she stood and the manner in which she composed her face. I reminded her of a situation at a local bagel store years earlier and she agreed that I probably just looked at the store workers, thought to myself that they displayed an utter lack of initiative, and didn't otherwise react. It's just how my faced looked [and hers, too].

The point of this story: if you wish to complain in person, be cognizant of the image you display. If you are like me or my children, both of whom have too much of my personality, you might want to try consciously to smile and to seem pleasant even if you are perturbed by something that just transpired.

There are good and useful etiquette points to remember if you are complaining in person. If you are standing, stand straight – don't slump. If offered an opportunity to shake hands, move your hand all the way to the webbing of the pro-offered hand. People in western countries like a firm handshake and, by moving to the webbing, neither of you can purposefully or accidentally hurt the other person. Don't chew gum. Turn off your cell phone so it won't ring - which is rude - and, worse, you won't be tempted to look at the text message or respond to the caller. Thank the individual when the conversation begins and thank him/her when the conversation ends. [And get yourself to a place where you can either write down or perhaps dictate into a cell phone a brief summary of what occurred, date, time, and location, so you have a record in case you need to pursue the situation likely in writing; don't rely on memory – there are too many studies of how faulty one's memory can be especially over time.]

If offered the opportunity to sit down, put your feet firmly on the floor; this will cause your rear end to move to the back of the chair and, correspondingly, you will lean forward about seven degrees. Psychologists like to say that this forward "lean" indicates you are interested in what the other individual is saying. This is far better than stretching out your legs, leaning backwards, crossing your arms, and giving an psychological indicator that you don't care and you are withdrawing from the situation. You don't want to slouch or look disinterested or bored or distracted. In either case, look the other person firmly in the eye. Remember, if possible, to smile unless your smile is unnatural. You want to present a friendly and certainly non-threatening demeanor.

Be sure to speak clearly. We all have accents, some are easily understood and some are not so easily understood. I speak very quickly; I realized that I can speak faster than many people can follow; I try to slow down, to note my points - "I have three points. First, there is . . . ." Speak up but with an "inside" voice; don't shout. One of my peeves about people and cell phones is that so many speak so loudly into their cell phones that everyone within ear shot becomes an unwillingly partner to the conversation. Don't whisper; don't shout; but speak with enough energy that your voice carries to the person either opposite you in person or listening to you on the telephone. If in person, watch hand gestures; they can be distracting. If you are so busy moving your hands with every phrase you speak, the listener might focus more on your hands than your words. When we were young, my father had my sister and me sit on our hands when speaking to learn to speak and to express ourselves using language and not hand gestures. Hand gestures were for emphasis, not simply accompaniment to the spoken word. It was tough at the time, but I appreciate that training now and for the past thirty-seven years in classrooms.

Whether you are speaking in person or over the telephone, watch out for slang and certainly for crude language. I am not "dude" whether on campus or in the community. I don't respond to crude language. I like to hear the occasional "please" and "thank you." Speak with courtesy or better yet don't use language you wouldn't use in front of your grandmother [unless your grandmother, like mine, never learned English so you could say what you wanted as long as you smiled and your father wasn't standing nearby ☺]. In some states, there is legislation that protects government employees from abuse, including verbal abuse; those laws are there for good reason.

Remember, if you insult people with whom you interacted, a good manager will feel obligated to defend them; you will have created a new impasse. Talk about the situation and not the people; keep the focus on actions people took and not the persons themselves. Good people make mistakes from time to time. If you seeking an informal resolution via personal contact, act as if it was a less-than-typical action for this company or organization; it will help the manager you are addressing to accept your points and move to the resolution you seek.

CHAPTER THIRTEEN

Complaining over the telephone

Of course, one may inquire or complain or seek resolution over the telephone. This is a kind of in-between an in-person complaint and a written letter. As with other kinds of complaints, inquiries, and suggestions, one must be organized, gathered the facts, arranged them into a compelling account, and be prepared to interact in real time with whoever is on the other end of the telephone. Always be polite; there is a person at the other end of the line who undoubtedly did not cause the situation about which you are calling; there is no excuse for rudeness or discourtesy and there certainly is no excuse for foul language. **If you know you have issues controlling**

your language when your emotions run higher, don't complain by telephone.

Besides needing to have notes for the telephone call, you need to decide ahead of time your purpose in calling. Do you simply want the organization to know of your displeasure? Do you want to exchange an item? Obtain a refund? Receive some kind of compensation for ill treatment?

Since you are on the telephone and not in person, it's a good idea to write out your points perhaps on note cards. In the old days of telephone interviews for faculty and administrative job openings, candidates – well, successful candidates! – would spread out 5"x8" note cards with a brief response for each of the typical questions that interview committees would ask. After all, there are only so many good job interview questions and it made sense to prepare an outline of one's responses – key points – ahead of time. One would make a brief comment as the beginning response to the interviewer's question, e.g., "I'm pleased to have an opportunity to discuss my philosophy of teaching," for example, and as one said that, one would reach for the card where one had a few bullet points and give a cogent, organized response. Skype® and other on-line software make it more obvious if you are reaching for that note card! But, if you are calling, you want to be organized – have notes or your major points written out in print large enough that you can easily read it while speaking over the telephone.

Finally, have a notepad available whether it is an old-fashioned paper notepad or a computer device. Write down the date and time of your call, the person who answered your call, and a rough summary of the contents of the conversation. As with an in-person discussion, such a written, contemporary record can prove valuable if you feel the need to complain further. It is hard to argue with a written record, assuming you take accurate notes.

As you probably have encountered, finding a "live" person who can help you can be difficult. Many phone lines lead the caller through a series of steps many of which seek to move you to an online site, a series of FAQs, or a box on an introductory web page in which you may type a comment, and definitely not towards a live person who can help you. Be persistent. Sometimes hitting the number "0" foils the phone answering system and it transfers you to an operator; sometimes speaking during the message, e.g., "representative, please" or "agent, please," achieves the same outcome. Realize that too many companies have so reduced staffing that finding a live person can be difficult and time consuming. And those people are likely overworked and as the day wears on, tired of hearing from upset customers.

Here's one that went incredibly easy. Several years ago I was reviewing our monthly credit card bill from our credit card provider, a wonderful company that serves those in the military and their families. I saw there was a charge for $999.99 – an unusual amount – for a purchase and a firm I could not identify. I called the company's toll-free number mostly to be sure I had the correct address to write to protest the charge and thereby retain my rights. Once I properly identified myself and the customer service representative checked our account, she said, "don't worry; we cancelled the charge." I asked should I write to preserve my rights, and she indicated she had cleared up the matter and I should deduct that charge when I paid our bill. Easy-peasy, as they say.

Here's another one that turned out well. Between Thanksgiving and Christmas 2012, I twice saw a commercial from one of the country's largest investment firms. It is a great firm, and we are among its millions of satisfied clients. A spokeswoman in the TV commercial noted that anyone who opened a new account and deposited a rather large sum would receive a $500 Apple® gift card. This was a very nice gift, indeed!

I admit I have this pet peeve about the value of new money compared to old or new business compared to existing business. Living in a college town, I see each June, as the next group of new students arrive for orientation, local banks offer fleece blankets, mugs, sweatshirts and other incentives to open a checking account to these new and temporary residents of our community [after all, we want them to graduate and move on]. Yet those same banks offer nothing to existing clients who remain with the bank for decades and who deposit far more money and keep far greater balances with the bank than typical first-year students.

Child-rearing experts always tell parents to tell well-behaved and well-acting children just how well they are doing so that these same children don't act badly just to attract attention. Some fast casual restaurants have loyalty programs where after so many purchases or so much money spent, the customer qualifies for a free cup of coffee, a soft drink, or a dessert. I think it is all variations on a theme.

Back in the days when only savings banks offered interest on personal savings accounts and the amount of interest paid was rather limited, there was a dodge of a sort practiced by little old ladies in East Coast and perhaps other cities. I say "little old ladies" because one of those was my Aunt Gussie, a real character, although there probably were little old men and some not so old women and men doing the same thing.

Savings banks in New York City would offer to pay interest from the tenth of the month for those months at the beginning of each quarter as if one had funds on deposit from the first of those months; separately, banks paid interest until the day of withdrawal. So these old ladies [again, there must have been some old men and some not –so-old ladies and men but I am using Aunt Gussie as my example] would go to their savings bank four times a year on the tenth of the month at the beginning of each quarter, withdraw all funds and collecting interest until that date of withdrawal, walk down the street, and open a new account at another savings bank and draw interest as if they had funds on deposit from the first day of that first month of the quarter – a gain of 40 days interest a year or an additional 9% on whatever the interest rate was, typically 4% per year compounded daily. Even as a teenager I wondered why these banks didn't offer some midpoint to retain the accounts; after all, my aunt would go from Bank A to Bank B in January and from Bank B back to Bank A or perhaps to Bank C and then again in April, July, and October. No bank really gained anything;

there was a lot of paperwork, and bank personnel spent a lot of time without really producing profit for the bank.

With this memory in my head, I was bothered enough by the investment company's ads that I dialed its toll-free number to speak with a representative at one of its investor service centers. I wasn't angry, but I had to explain why the ad bothered me. I realized in talking to a very nice, very polite company employee that she didn't care all that much; she likely had never fielded such a telephone call before. She just wanted to give me my hearing.

So I followed up by writing a letter – my favorite way to complain – to the company CEO although in the nearly two years since he recently stepped down from that position as managing head of the company. I noted the advertisement; my issue of why new money was worth so much more than additional funds by existing clients [the child playing nicely] and recounted the story of my aunt and others in New York City in the 1950s and 1960s. I wondered why the investment firm didn't offer something but not as much as the $500 Apple gift card to existing clients who invested the same amount of new funds in an existing account compared to new clients investing that amount in new accounts. I even had the temerity to suggest the idea of a $25 or $50 gift card from a major retailer or casual restaurant chain.

From the prompt response I received, one can see one of the reasons why this investment firm has been such a great success. The president and CEO had an assistant call me at work; he told me that his boss liked my letter; he remembered the bank switching as I described it, and wanted to offer me a reward of a sort for my letter. That was great. And, of course, I have told so many people that, with any luck, the company has gained in new investments and the legitimate management fee it charges on such mutual fund investments far more than the amount the CEO kindly offered me.

Still, it took a letter and not only a telephone call.

I have another example with a not dissimilar outcome. Several years ago we decided to step up to the plate and get cell phones. Whoopee. And, as I noted earlier, several years later we wanted to take advantage of an offer from our cellular telephone carrier, T-Mobile, to get new phones and a new plan [and I noted the problem we had with the rebate which T-Mobile kindly resolved to our satisfaction].

It so happens that my wife, Ann, signed up for the plan; I was a family member on her plan. Well, neither of us is the most technologically proficient individual and we had some issues with the telephone. The cell phone company apparently arranged with third parties to offer services to cell phone plan holders. And one day in trying to "unlock" the telephone, I apparently and absolutely accidentally wound up signing up for one of these third party services. I didn't want it. I called the company's customer service office to complain. While I could sign up for a new service whether purposefully or accidentally, I could not cancel it because I was not the account holder of record. This stupefied me. The company's representative said she could not speak with me. In theory, a minor child could push buttons and sign up for a service yet only the parent could cancel it? When the cell phone "unlocked," it apparently unlocked in a message from one of these third party service providers and I accidentally accepted an offer I didn't want nor realized I had taken.

I wrote my typical letter, explained all of this, indicated I could not imagine the circumstances where I cared about these third party services, criticized the corporate policy that I could sign up for something which I could not cancel – I wondered about its legality, and insisted that the company reverse the charges and cancel any of these unwanted services. It took several letters and later several follow-up telephone calls from the company to straighten out the situation; we have cell phones which are blocked for all third party services, which, had a company representative asked when we first signed up for cell phone service, we would have requested.

I tried calling; I reverted to writing a letter – putting everything and everyone on record and creating a paper trail that I value having.

For some months running, I saw a TV commercial for a company advertising software that automatically calculates and affixes postage to any kind of package a company or individual wants to mail. One of the actors in the commercial said "there's nothing worse than standing in line at the post office" as part of a testimonial for this company and its software that permits users to print postage right from their computer. That sounds great - a real time saver – but there are "things" that are worse than standing in line at the post office.

My sister, Debbie, fought and lost a valiant, sixteen month battle with ovarian cancer. It dragged her down into the depths of hell but she climbed out and we proclaimed victory; then, several months later, it returned and she never got ahead. It was sad - for her husband of nearly forty years, her daughters, our mother, me, and her many friends.

As you may imagine, that commercial bothered me. The company didn't mean harm, but whoever designed the commercial went a bit too far. Why needlessly upset viewers who, if nothing else, would react by never using that company's products. So, I called the toll-free number and explained my views. The service representative was nice, but made no promises. To the great credit of the company, it changed the commercial. Thank you very, very much!

Sometimes the call doesn't go so well. Recently, we received a letter addressed to a "John Dobbs" from a collection agency located in a city in northwest Iowa. I am not related to anyone named John Dobbs. I opened the letter and worried about a mistake; I assume someone named John Dobbs did incur the debt for which the agency was seeking payment; I assume his last listed address may well have been in Ames, Iowa where we lived; I was willing to bet that someone working at the collection agency checked addresses in Ames for anyone with the last name of Dobbs, Ann or I likely were the first Dobbsses [yes, this is the plural of "Dobbs" as strange as it may look!] listed alphabetically, and the agency sent the letter to our address. I worried that somehow this debt might find its way to our credit rating.

I called the agency; a receptionist transferred me to another employee. I explained the situation and got nowhere. I described what I thought occurred and I wanted a letter stating clearly that we were not the subject of this debt collection. She refused. She claimed her firm never did that. I asked her for the name of the firm's owner; when she initially declined, I mentioned I could likely find it through the Better Business Bureau or Chamber of Commerce in Sioux City and she gave it to me.

I wrote the owner, stated more firmly than normal the situation as I perceived it, his employee's uncooperative attitude, and made clear my demand for a written statement that we were clear of this debt collection. I also commented on his employee's rudeness and lack of helpfulness based on my written notes of the conversation. He responded quickly with a letter as I requested. Firmness is okay; impoliteness is not.

Back to an Iowa winter day. Universities rarely close because of weather. First, the idea of "closing" is a misnomer. Institutions still need to deliver heat and electricity to residence halls, maintain computer facilities, and there are laboratories, experiments, animals, etc. even if institutions cancel classes. Students complain about having to go to class in bad weather but that is life in the northern United States; companies can't regularly close throughout the winter. All too often if a kind-hearted college or university president does decide to cancel classes for the day [or the afternoon or the evening], frequently bars in the areas surrounding that particular campus report record business from students who were too cold to go to class but not to visit local drinking establishments ☺!

As happened several times each winter in Iowa, there was a bad storm. A student called the President's Office in the morning to demand that we cancel classes. I explained the process . . . that around 4:30 am the president, the business vice president, the campus police chief, the city chief of police, the director of the combined city/university bus company all join in a conference call to discuss road conditions. Basically, if the bus system determined its buses can get through the streets, the university holds classes. And that particular morning all agreed buses could navigate their routes around town.

That wasn't the answer he wanted, and he began swearing at me and threatening me. Nowadays that's a stupid reaction. It is too easy to note the telephone number and in the worst case to turn it over to the police. It showed he was a boor. Still, this situation occurred too often during my years of being first in the office and hence first to answer the telephone.

One time someone called the President's Office at night. Obviously, no one was there to receive the call. The caller left an expletive-laden voice mail for the president but, and I think he should have known this, he left the message on the president's secretary's telephone. She was offended. She listened to the message and asked me to come to her desk, handed me the telephone and played it. I was shocked. I contacted the campus police, and the director of public safety called the caller, a student at the University, read him the riot act, and insisted he apologize, as we agreed, not just to the president but to this very nice woman who was the president's executive secretary, and who did not deserve to listen to such foul language on her telephone.

CHAPTER FOURTEEN

Last Resorts

Use Social Media

Okay, you've done your best. You have gathered information, organized your thoughts, made a cogent argument, got the "ear" of a significant administrator, and received no satisfaction. Is there anything else you can do?

It depends on your sense of aggrievement and your need for resolution and/or satisfaction. As one who remembers telephones with cords, televisions with channel dials, manual typewriters, and all other sorts of once important but now largely outdated technology, I am not attuned to the social media of today. However, many companies and organizations have one or more employees or even an office dedicated to monitoring social media sites. You may wish to create a social media site or file a comment – write out your story or cut-and-paste the letter[s] you have written. There is a very good chance that the company or organization will respond to you rather than face criticism on such a blog and perhaps a concomitant loss of business because of your account of your dealings.

A wise communications professor at my previous institution always told her classes and young faculty intelligent enough to listen that all communication is one way. It's one thing perhaps to be a little too tough, perhaps a little too rough directly to a corporate or institutional representative, but having such language posted onto a social media site is there for everyone to see. Before posting anything, have a friend read over what you intend to post; make sure you won't regret the posting after it goes "live."

Contact the Better Business Bureau

You can always contact the Better Business Bureau or the Chamber of Commerce either where you received the service or where the company or organization has its headquarters. Some people do check with the BBB to see if there are such complaints although I suspect more check social media.

If you wish to follow this route, you need to visit the Better Business Bureau website or the website of a local affiliate. If you go to the national site, it asks for your zip code to direct you to that local website. I checked several local websites, and they are similar. You need to determine that your complaint fits a category the BBB seeks to resolve. The site will ask you for information – the company, its location, the nature of your issue, etc.

Please remember that the BBB receives many complaints – hundreds if not thousands in the course of a few days and so it will take a while for a response. As the BBB website notes, "everything you submit will be forwarded to the business within two business days. . . . You will be notified of the business's response when we receive it (or notified that we received no response)" That last phrase is critical; the BBB has no power to compel a business to respond; it seeks to persuade but if the company or organization refused to respond to your reasonable entreaties, assuming they were reasonable, it might also not respond to a follow-up from the BBB. It also may conclude that the business has done its best to resolve the issue and thus not follow-up on the consumer's filing. Finally, realize that the various BBB affiliates function on dues that businesses pay; this does not mean there is a conflict of interest but it does put a BBB investigator or mediator in a difficult position between the consumer complaining and the business whose dues financially underwrite the BBB affiliate. Nonetheless, the various BBB affiliates claim they resolve some 70 percent of the complaints they receive, which is a high percentage, but they don't indicate in whose favor.

Your respective State Attorney General's Consumer Protection Unit

You may also check out the consumer protection unit of your state Attorney General's office. In Iowa, it is the Consumer Protection Division; it is similarly named in other states. As with the Better Business Bureau, I checked the websites for several states' attorneys general and not surprisingly they are similar. While there is a unit in each AG's office that receives consumer complaints, the web sites for each office seeks to direct consumers to specific state and federal agencies that are better equipped or more appropriate to handle the matter. If you do follow-up with these agencies it means you likely have a serious complaint and suffered some serious wrong – injury, loss of large assets, etc. – and perhaps you should begin by consulting an attorney in your city for advice on how best to proceed. Paying for an hour of time of a qualified, experienced attorney can be a great investment if you are determined to see the matter to closure.

Sue in Small Claims Court

You can sue in small claims court. The small claims court system is relatively new, reaching only back to the 1960s. These courts have jurisdiction over private disputes that do not involve a lot of money; a claimant does not need an attorney but also waives the right to claim more than the court can award. In Iowa, for example, there is a $5,000 maximum award. Small claims court judges oversee a system with more simplified rules, based on the assumption that individuals should be able to represent themselves without benefit of legal counsel. Please note that many courts encourage both parties to settle or engage a third party mediator rather than use the small claims court route.

If you wish to pursue your case in small claims court, go to the court in the district where the case arose; check with the Clerk's Office for that court for a "small claims" handbook that cites the rules for small claims in your jurisdiction. There is no federal small claims court, so there are at least 51 [including the District of Columbia] separate jurisdictions.

Once you have read through the handbook, follow instructions. You will need to file a summons and complaint and provide necessary information including the person or persons, company or companies you are suing, a valid working address, and the amount you are seeking [remembering the typical $5,000 limit]. You have to "serve" the complaint yourself which typically means sending a copy by certified mail or engaging a process server which costs more. Obviously show up on time, neatly dressed, and prepared to present your case at the time and date the court notes. Remember, the judge has many cases to hear and often you will be limited to fifteen minutes; practice ahead of time standing in front of a mirror; be organized; be reasonable; be detailed; be polite. When it is time for the business owner or representative to speak, listen politely. DON'T EVER INTERRUPT. Don't think what you see in television courtroom dramas hold. Instead, make a note and when the judge asks you to react, give your evidence to him or her to disprove whatever seemed incorrect to you. The judge may render a judgment immediately or take the case under advisement; in the latter situation, you will receive a written judgment.

And, finally, if you are committed to seeing the complaint through to its denouement, you may hire an attorney and seek legal redress. This is an action of the last resort; it usually means you have suffered a grievous loss or injury, and are not satisfied by the company's offer of compensation. As a college faculty member, I live in a collegial world; lawyers exist in an adversarial environment. Once you engage an attorney, you have changed the tenor of the conversation. If that's the path you wish to follow, good luck.

Check with your local bar association for a list of attorneys who specialize in the area of law that covers your complaint. You may wish to check with several to find one who can best represent you.

CHAPTER FIFTEEN

A Final Word

Okay . . . you now have the basics before you. You can continue to complain to friends, the bathroom mirror, or your family pet and gain little satisfaction.

You can be boorish and yell at people who have done nothing to deserve your anger and do **not** have the authority to help resolve the matter in a satisfactory manner to you.

You can simply internalize your disappointment and over time that will likely eat away at you. There aren't enough antacids in the world to neutralize that frustration.

Or you can practice organizing and writing a compelling, convincing letter to the organizational leadership and gain some satisfaction.

I believe we are engaging in a good thing, to help companies and organizations improve their operations, to provide CEOs with feedback on problems that otherwise they would not receive, and thus to help strengthen business and bureaucracy with which we all deal on a daily basis.

Please sign up for this worthy effort. I have created a blog where we can post our successes, our failures, and ask other blog readers for advice. I will moderate this blog for language - no foul language and perhaps mostly good grammar - and for content - companies and organizations have a right to fair treatment - so no unfair accusations and certainly no threats.

If you have successes to share, please write me; I am looking forward to hearing from you.

Good luck!

CHARLES M. DOBBS